Reviewer's C

"The often unhealthy aspects of organisational life
practical approaches to addressing these in a s
needed helping hand to bring an often daunting
leaders, managers, practitioners and anyone with
more effectively."

Graham Barkus, Head of Organisation Development and Learning,
Cathay Pacific Airways

"This book makes a valuable contribution and is consistent with the values of effective and authentic leadership. The worked examples are extremely helpful and I wish I had them many years ago. It caused me to reflect and that's what is really important about any such text – you learn and gain insight."

Tony Bell OBE, Chief Executive,
Liverpool and Broadgreen Hospitals NHS Trust

"This book helps managers to identify not just what needs to be done 'in the moment', but also how open and honest discussion between employees and employers can lead to what Mike Wash describes as 'organisational healing'. Though many of the situations and dialogues are fun to read, they also make the reader squirm with embarrassment from the sheer recollection of having heard these types of conversations before – and yet, done little to bring about learning and renewal in any real or meaningful way. *54 Approaches to Organisational Healing* illustrates clearly what it takes to sustain health and wealth through the process of work."

Christopher Bunker, Head of HR Europe,
Polaroid Corporation (part of the Petters Group Worldwide)

"Mike Wash developed this approach to organisational healing over a number of years in conjunction with a multitude of clients and through the pages of this book provides a very personal, challenging and supportive approach into effective ways of constructively challenging the status quo and making difficult issues discussable. The tools and techniques in this book can help you to resource a healthy future, improve organisational performance and establish a very human culture of 'the way we do things around here'."

George Buchanan, Chief Executive,
(Retired)

"Mike Wash uses his vast experience of people, organisations and processes to enable the reader to enhance themselves, their organisations and their lives. This book will be invaluable for CEO's, MD's, coaches and anyone working, needing or choosing to heal their organisation. I shall recommend this to all my students as absolutely essential reading."

Dr Graham Dexter, Module Leader,
University of Hull Coaching Masters Course

"An excellent guide to assist organisations to help people reach a state where work becomes a healthy, balanced aspect of life, and the organisation grows as a sustainable creator of wealth."

Dr Paul Donaldson, Chairman,
Sysco Management Consultants Limited

"This book presents a really useful challenge to every manager and leader, no matter how long they have been in business. I would recommend this to anyone brave enough to admit they are not perfect!"

Suzanne Hughes, Regional Corporate Affairs Manager,
Environment Agency – North West UK

"I wish that I had access to this insightful book when I was a young manager who knew everything (!), but needed reference points and a counter-view. Come to think of it, I wish that I'd had it when I was an old manager!"

Lawrence Jackson, Managing Director (Retired),
Gentech International Limited

"Mike Wash is insightful, caring, realistic and yet visionary. He wants you to make the best of the world and the people you find in it. If you believe in working together healthily for continuous improvement then this book is for you. It tells you how to achieve it and how to spot mistakes you might be making. As ever, he writes clearly, with passion and yet with practicality. I wish he was my manager."

Lindsey Jackson, Director,
Enhance Wellbeing Limited

"Having used the approaches described within this resource, and seen the benefits for individuals, team and the organisation as a result, I would say this is a must-have resource for any organisation development practitioner. Mike brings the subject matter to life in a very practical way."

Alison Johnson, Assistant Director of Organisation Development,
Halton and St Helens Primary Care Trust

"Once again, Mike Wash provides telling insights from his great practical experience in identifying the symptoms shown by unhealthy organisations and guiding them towards a healthy future."

Professor Tom McGuffog MBE

"Mike Wash is the kind of person who helps others to reach inside, find hidden resources, pull them out and point them in the right direction, to produce great results in life and business. In this rich and accessible book he helps the reader to understand the principles of how to work in an effective, ethical and holistic way – if you work in any kind of human resources – you will want to read this book now!"

Dr Janice Russell, Module Leader,
University of Hull Coaching Masters Course

"This has all the most useful tools in the essential tool kit for someone new to the notion of manager as facilitator. This is essential organisational first aid to enable organisations to move toward greater health."

Bryce Taylor, Director,
Oasis School of Human Relations

54 APPROACHES TO ORGANISATIONAL HEALING

To Nick – best wishes
Great to meet up again!.

Michael Wash

- 'From crisis to turnaround'
- 'From mediocrity to sustainable business excellence'
- 'How to create fulfilment at work'

2000

For a complete list of Management Books 2000 titles
visit our web-site on http://www.mb2000.com

First published in 2009 by Management Books 2000 Ltd
Forge House, Limes Road
Kemble, Cirencester
Gloucestershire, GL7 6AD, UK
Tel: 0044 (0) 1285 771441
Fax: 0044 (0) 1285 771055
Email: info@mb2000.com
Web: www.mb2000.com

British Library Cataloguing in Publication Data is available

ISBN 9781852526153

To all my clients and friends who have helped me shape my experiences and;
hence – shaped this book.

Acknowledgements

I have had the good fortune and opportunity to consult to and train people all over the world. This would not have been possible without the loving and professional support from my wife; Mave.

My past clients who have been invaluable in giving me constructive and supportive feedback. In particular; George Buchanan, Tony Bell, Alison Johnson, Graham Higgins, Graham Barkus, Chris Bunker, Suzanne Hughes and Lawrence Jackson.

Contents

Introduction

Very often, organisations embark upon programmes of change and improvement. This may be as a result of a crisis, a need for turnaround, change in leadership or a demand from 'on high' regarding policy or political change.

Whatever the reason, these programmes of change are unsustainable as programmes, just as a diet is a quick fix for losing weight, joining a gym to get fit, or swotting for an exam to get qualifications. They are all short term 'flavours of the month' and without a longer-term, value-based strategy will die off until the next fad appears.

Too often, organisations seek 'treatment' rather than 'cure'. They opt for training, re-engineering, structure change, imposition of new targets, management consultants. Organisations have been doing this for years, and they will continue to get what they have always got – short term success.

Opting for a cure, rather than a treatment, requires Leadership to embark upon the path of creating a 'healing organisation'. A healing organisation changes its way of life so that it becomes self sustainable, naturally growing healthier because its value base is in the hearts and minds of everyone who works there. Everyone cares and everyone benefits, as they grow healthier out of a blueprint or DNA of excellence which is the core of the organisation's genetic identity.

54 Approaches to Organisational Healing explores best practice for sustainable excellence, proposing radical, challenging and creative approaches to becoming the best at what you do. In this book, there is a strong analogy between our attitude to our own personal health and well-being, and our attitude towards the way we behave at work.

Organisations have predominantly been seen as mechanistic structures to manipulate and mould according to the whims and demands of their leaders and customers. By acknowledging the organisation as a living organism, we can clearly and significantly relate personal health to organisational health.

All organisations have some aspect of 'disease'. Ignoring this disease process can lead to institutionalised dysfunction, substandard service, stress at work and the inevitable loss of business and/or increase in customer/consumer complaints.

Introducing models and processes, investing in training and education, or using smart or lean tools and techniques is not enough to sustain health. These approaches need to be introduced on a firm foundation of a 'healthy organisation vision', underpinned by strongly held beliefs and values about how people should be 'treated' at work.

Organisational Healing is the process of developing the organisation to achieve a state where the people, processes, systems and policies are sustainable and consistent with achieving a continuously improving healthy state of being.

A 'Healing Organisation' is an organisation with a culture of self-sustaining continuous improvement which achieves the best quality of service, outcome or product. In doing so, it creates a healthy and fulfilling work environment for everyone.

Is this book for you?

This book is particularly useful for those people in a position where they want to make a difference, and firmly believe they can – a difference that goes beyond the purpose of work. Often, this occurs when you are in, or intend to be in, a position that has the potential for improving people's lives through the process of a 'healthy work environment' – and in doing this, achieving sustainable business excellence.

Do you lead an organisation, department or team? Are you involved in facilitating a programme of change? Are you a member of a project team attempting to improve and change the way people work? Do you want to know how organisations can change for the better? If the answer to these questions is yes, you might, from time to time, find yourself considering the following points.

What does it take to create sustainable excellence?

Imagine every individual in the organisation caring passionately about what they do, as if they owned the organisation themselves.

What if you had the reputation where, year on year, new levels of productivity, quality and service were achieved and you had the best people getting even better?

What if responsible leadership was about providing vision and direction with a light touch to a trusted team to get on with it?

Is it possible to create an organisation whose boundaries and networks extend beyond its own core processes, bringing learning and support to the wider community – thus creating a presence that adds value and nurtures public and customer loyalty?

If you are interested in these kinds of questions, if you are the kind of person who can see potential for improvement and increased fulfilment within your business values, then this book is for you.

It is a great read for anyone wanting to make a difference in their organisation. Whether you are the Chief Executive, a manager, a change agent or a member of a project team, you will recognise, enjoy and learn from the descriptions of the trials, tribulations and reality which typify whole-system organisational change.

How to use this book

The 54 Approaches to Organisational Healing are highlighted in the body of the text (see page 24 for the first). These approaches are not discreet and are part of an integral process of organisational development. For the busy manager wishing to dip into particular aspects, I have listed the 54 Approaches in the next section. Whether you are about to embark upon, or are in the process of, a change programme, you may have a question related to one of the approaches identified. This will help focus your reading.

There is a fictional tale at the beginning of each chapter which provides a sequential read and indicates the importance of designing and implementing organisation-wide changes on solid foundations. While the company and its employees are fictional, the characters and incidents have been shaped by real life examples I have come across during my consultancy assignments over the last 20 years. The events described have largely been shaped by my experiences in the Health Sector and other service industries.

The tale is based on a medium-sized manufacturing and distribution business in the North of England. Each Chapter gives a snapshot of organisational life through the relationships between the Managing Director, his team and key incidents that challenge that state of 'organisational health'.

After each work based story, our Managing Director, Dave Battle, gains relief from stress by playing golf with his friend, Ged Shaw, who happens to be a retired Management Consultant. It is amazing what new insights and parallels can be made when playing golf or indeed any time out of a work situation where play and creativity can flourish.

Bringing creativity and insights back to the workplace is the challenge.

The book can be read and used in a number of different ways, depending on the readers' needs and interest. If an overview of what it takes to introduce a system-wide development process is needed then a sequential journey through each chapter may be the best option. If there are particular areas of weakness or 'disease' in your organisation that you want to strengthen, then focusing or particular 'approaches' or chapters can help. If you wish to understand the role of manager as a facilitator, then Chapter 4 is particularly useful.

54 Approaches Summarised

The Healing Organisation –
The 7 Elements

The 54 Approaches to Organisational Healing are contained within 7 key elements of the 'Healing Organisation'.

To achieve Healing Organisation status requires alignment of the seven elements. These are:

1. Awareness

Being open to learning and receiving feedback, to understand the impact that you and your team have on each other and everyone else. Realising your personal and team power to influence the life of the organisation and the lives within it.

2. Leadership – Channelling Personal Power

Applying your interpersonal skills to helping others become more effective at what they do. Coaching others to manage change, improvement and problem solve effectively. Developing this ability at every level within the organisation.

3. Connectedness

Developing a one-team, holistic and inclusive communication philosophy, which develops a mutual respect and trust across all departments and levels.

4. Ownership

Every individual taking initiative to improve their own work situation. This is supported, recognised and rewarded. Each individual continuously searching for new ideas, ways of preventing mistakes or improving quality and enjoying the challenge of continuous change.

5. Belief

Creating an excitement and passion for what you and your organisation stand for. An environment where people want to buy into the organisation's purpose and values because it offers an opportunity to grow, to realise ambition and dreams

6. Nourishment

Taking care of your people by ensuring they have access to the best information, technology and facilities in order to be efficient and healthy at work.

7. Cure

Take the medicine by all means, but ensure the organisation is on the path of adopting a healthier lifestyle. Confront the discrepant or diseased part, utilise creative and alternative methods to tap into the ability of the organisation to self-heal and achieve long-lasting sustainable business excellence.

1

Awareness

My proposition to you, right now, is that you are having a significant impact on the people you live and work with, in ways that you may not always be aware of.

Through your behaviour, and the words you speak, a dramatic chain of events occur. Some of this may be intentional; most of it is unknown. The ripple effect of our influence goes beyond any immediate interaction to create a momentum of unstoppable change. We do not realise how powerful we are.

Take Dave Battle for example; the new Managing Director of Delectrex Limited.

Delectrex Limited

Dave Battle was somewhat disappointed at not having found a reserved parking space for his new 7-Series BMW, especially as he felt – as the new Managing Director – he should be able to park close to his office.

Eventually, after squeezing in between two less grand vehicles around the back of the office block, he walked up to reception. He noticed the grubby appearance of the furniture, out of date displays and the musty smell – a mixture of dampness and oil. The greeting from Thelma was, well . . . .

"Now chuck, what can I do for ya?" Thelma squawked loudly with a broad, over-lip-glossed smile.

Dave replied "I'm Mr Battle, the new Managing Director."

"Really! Well, no-one tells me owt these days love – welcome to the funny farm – it's crazy some days. Do I need to give you a badge or something or shall I ring Babs, the last MD's secretary?" Dave nodded, noting Thelma's well meaning but over-informal style; he would have to deal with that later.

"No, that's fine, I think I remember where the office is – I'll go straight up."

Quickly exiting through the doors marked 'Staff Only' and up the well-worn brown carpeted stairs, flanked by metal railings with chipped yellow peeling paint, he began to wonder what surprises lay ahead.

Entering into his secretary's office; "Good morning, Barbara."

"Oh, good morning, sir." she responded politely. She sounded nervous.

Good, much better, Dave thought, just what he liked. "That's OK – call me Mr Battle."

"Yes sir, oh er, I mean – Mr Battle – can I get you a tea or . . . .?"

"Coffee, black – no sugar – real stuff, not the instant rubbish." Dave spoke with authority, starting as he meant to go on.

"Yes Mr Battle, right away. On your desk, sir, is an itinerary left by Mrs Hart, our Personnel Director and Mr Acton, our Operations Director."

"I'll sort out my own itinerary, thank you. Can you get hold of the Finance Director please – Mr McKavit I think – I'd like to see him straight away. Also, I'd like to call a full executive team meeting at, say, 11am – that gives them a good couple of hours to prepare."

"Shall I say what it's about?"

"The fact I have called a meeting should be enough Barbara – thank you. Oh, and by the way – find out what needs to be done to get me a reserved parking space outside the front entrance."

And with that, Dave nodded curtly and made his way to his office. As he went in, he wondered whether 'Babs', who, with her dyed blonde hair and grey roots and somewhat old fashioned cardigan, looked like she should be at home knitting for her grandchildren, would be able to cope with what he considered to be his demanding but fair style of management.

Dave settled into his leather office chair and swivelled nonchalantly around, surveying his newly acquired empire.

His office overlooked the car park – handy for seeing the comings and goings and the late comers. Excellent! It was a good sized office with inspirational posters on the wall: 'Energy and Resistance will conquer all', 'Cherish your vision and your dreams' and 'Teamwork – there is no better energy for your heart than reaching out and lifting people up'.

The carpet looked a bit worn, but the Board table looked old and grand enough to match the aspiring status of the new MD.

He was excited and anticipated achieving great things with this newly acquired sense of authority and control.

* * * * *

"Ah – Mr McKavit – Richard . . . ."

"Dick actually – Welcome to Delectrex – how can I help you?" Dick was always helpful, diligent and pedantic. He was 6' 1" and thin as a rake, yet he didn't believe he warranted the name 'lean and mean'.

"I want you to go over the last 3 years' results and bring me up to date with today's figures."

"Sure, no problem. Will tomorrow do? It will give me time to prepare."

"What's wrong with now? Surely they are all accessible on the system?" Dave stuck to his guns of starting as he meant to go on – *aim high, demand more and see what happens!*

"Yes, but I prefer to have a hard copy and I will need to print the appropriate summaries and forecasts off."

"Then get on with it, Dick. I need to get up to date before the meeting at 11am. So, let's say – half an hour . . . ."

"Well, er . . . ."

"Good, see you then."

Ha! Don't give them room to make excuses.

Dick sheepishly turned to go, but he wasn't getting off that easily.

"Oh, by the way, I assume we have a budget to redecorate this office. It's looking very dated and we need to make a good impression on visitors."

Dick, now a little red-faced, replied, "I'll have a look."

"Good – see you in half an hour."

*   *   *   *   *

Forty-five minutes later, Dick, still red-faced, took a deep breath having rushed through an overview of the company's financial situation.

"So, what you're telling me Dick is that for the past 3 years, our profits have reduced by 20%, losing 5% year on year. Sales are stable, no growth, costs are up, returns have increased and projections are poor – what's going on?"

"Well, this is quite complex really."

"Try me!"

"Last year, we had a strike and . . . ."

*   *   *   *   *

Babs made sure her door was shut before making the 'urgent' phone calls.

"Hello, Daphne Hart!"

"Hi Daphne, the big chief is here. Well – not that big really – rather more small and stout! Anyway – he wants a full team meeting at 11am."

"Oh, hello Babs – 11am? That's a bit short notice, I have appointments all day – can't we shift it to the end of the day?"

"He's very insistent – it seems urgent!"

"Oh dear, that sounds imminent – didn't he read the itinerary – we put in a team meeting scheduled for Wednesday."

"No – he wants to design his own itinerary."

"Oh, OK – I'll be there."

*   *   *   *   *

"Doreen Deli!" The M54 was a dangerous distraction.

"Doreen? Hi, it's Babs – Mr Battle wants a meeting this morning at 11am."

"Ridiculous – I'm on my way to a Marketing Conference – give my apologies."

"Are you on hands-free?"

"Yes – of course." One-handed actually, as she took another puff of her cigarette.

"Well, he seemed very insistent and it seems very important."

"It means me turning around – I might just make it by 11am!"

"Good – I'll tell him you're on the way."

*   *   *   *   *

"It's five past eleven Barbara – where is Dan?" Dave began to show a little impatience.

"Erm, I did tell him – he was on the shop floor dealing with a conveyor belt breakdown problem."

"Ring please – tell him we are all waiting for him. Meanwhile – let's have a coffee – Daphne – you play Mother."

Dan walked in – still drying his hands.

"Ah, Dan – good of you to join us. Let's get started. Thanks for coming, I must say, however, one of my pet hates is poor punctuality. In future – all of our meetings will start on time."

Dan replied with some frustration "If we don't get the belt started soon, we miss at least a thousand orders. It's a priority."

"This is a priority, Dan." Once again, Dave asserted his authority.

Dan bit his lip, knowing full well he would need to give the new boss a chance, particularly as he was harbouring disappointment at not getting the MD position himself.

"Right – I would like to hear, from each of you, why this business seems to be going from bad to worse?"

Doreen – Sales and Marketing:

"Well, despite us losing one of our best customers last year, we seem to be coping. The new product marketing information was late and we have lost a few good external salesmen. There's also a problem with the new order-processing system, which makes it difficult for the telesales team."

Dan – Operations:

"The conveyor belt is old, antiquated and breaks down daily! The Stores are not up-to-date, order-filling processes are inaccurate due to poor supervision and general tardiness."

Dick – IT and Finance:

"It takes a while for new systems to bed in – I don't know why we are having problems. I'd have to get my IT manager in to report on this. As far as Finance is concerned – auditors are happy – books balance, and people are sticking to their budgets."

Daphne – Personnel:

"We have staff-side relationship problems. Never really recovered from last year's strike. Sickness and absence is high. Morale has improved since we had the Christmas party – despite the couple of arrests after the brawl and the sexual harassment accusation – which I should be dealing with this morning. Generally though, we are an efficient department coping with a high demand for support."

Dave couldn't believe his ears! To him, these were excuses communicated in such a way as if they were not a problem, a job to do, the norm, crises – what crises?!

He could see a firm hand was going to be needed here. Strong leadership and probably heads will roll!!

*   *   *   *   *

"Here's your pint, Ged – you played well, although my game was way off today."

Ged Shaw was a long-standing friend and golf partner of Dave's. Their regular Saturday morning golf game was also a good opportunity to catch up, but mainly for Dave to 'whinge' about work!

"Yes, I just couldn't get my mid-range fairway shots to work at all!"

"Hmmm – you did seem to be punching them a bit more than usual – and it's unusual for you to give up on a hole despite getting lost in the woods."

"Yeah – I guess work was still interfering with the game."

"First week huh? Good one?"

"You're joking – disaster! You wouldn't believe it!"

"Try me."

Dave told Ged how his first team meeting went and then he elaborated on how his tour of the warehouse and other departments was a real eye-opener and a good opportunity to start improving things. He described the helpful suggestions he had made as he went round: clean up reception, clean up the canteen, reorganise the desks in the open-plan telesales office, make more signposting, improve security, install coffee facilities for waiting guests and so on.

"I thought the week had gone well – until I had my secretary in the office in tears with her resignation, the operations director, Dan bawling me out and accusing me of not understanding the business and, to cap it all, another threatened strike next week! To be honest Ged, I'm beginning to wonder if I've taken on too much!"

"Mmmm," Ged looked thoughtful and paused slightly before asking his good friend a question: "How do you think the people you dealt with this week feel about you?"

Dave replied and sounded slightly irritated. "Oh – here we go – psychobabble consultancy – look Ged – I'm there to do a job, not to run a welfare programme."

"Wow – that hit a nerve. You're still angry. It's a fair question. I'll ask it another way – what impact did you want to have on the people who would be working for you?"

Ged had been, in his younger days, a high-flying business consultant. Despite his balding and somewhat overweight appearance, and his nonchalant laid-back manner, he could still convey the occasional wise question leading to insightful reflection.

"I don't know, Ged, I never thought about it. All I know is that one of the reasons Barbara – or Babs as everyone calls her – gives for her wanting to leave is that she gets all the complaints about the changes following the suggestions I made." Dave snorted. "They were only suggestions."

"What do you mean?"

"When I pointed out the lax security in the place, we got an accusation of changing job roles without consulting reception staff, grievance from the staff side because a short-cut route to the canteen has been blocked off and an accusation that because my office and the guest waiting area is being decorated, the new boss is not in touch with reality. Then I was given an invitation to visit the warehouse toilets – which, by the way – were a real eye-opener!!"

"You don't seem to have a clear picture of how you impact others. I just wonder how much you know about yourself, your personal power and the ability to match intention with reality." Ged caught himself and stopped short – consultant speak again!

"I probably need a good consultant, eh Ged!"

"Don't look at me – my days of working miracles are over." Ged smiled. "Fancy another pint?"

"No – I'd better get off. Got a lot to think about, and I promised the wife I would cut the lawn. See you next week."

"You bet."

As you can see, within his first week, Mr Dave Battle of Delectrex Limited, had antagonised his own team and created industrial unrest throughout the company, all through his good intentions to improve things! Dave has clearly neglected his personal development through the years in the area of 'self-awareness', failing to understand how his own personal style impacts others, or the potential to adapt it to suit the occasion.

This Chapter explains a variety of ways to do this and invites readers to take an honest look at themselves, their style of management and hence leadership potential and responsibility.

Within this element of 'Awareness', the following principles are explored:

- Know yourself and your purpose.
- Act with respect and sensitivity.
- Realise the power of choice.
- Be open.
- Open up the opportunity for leadership.
- Creating positive awareness.

Know yourself and your purpose

The simplest questions are often the most powerful – for example, who are you, what do you want, what's your purpose, what are you trying to achieve, what's really important to you?

If you can answer these questions reasonably quickly, with deep sincerity, because you have thought about the answers for quite some time, then you are well on your way to knowing the 'directional' sense of who you are. This is only part of the mystery, for our lives and our circumstances are forever changing, therefore these reflective questions tantalise our sense of purpose whenever we are at a threshold of change or in a dilemma about direction.

> **1. Understand how your own personal style impacts others, and its potential to be adapted to suit the occasion.**

In the story of our new MD, Dave Battle is described as a man who seems to be very clear about his purpose. To him there seems nothing more important than to get the company making ever increasing profits. He begins to take full responsibility personally, offering quick-fired solutions to all around him. Unfortunately, little does he realise that his sense of purpose is not shared. At some point, he will have to realise that he cannot turn this company round on his own. Knowing your 'directional self' or having a clear sense of purpose is equally important to everyone. It's particularly important for those in a leadership position with a responsibility of 'directing' an organisation towards success. However, if an organisation wants to achieve continuous, sustainable success then *every* individual's sense of contribution and value needs to be congruent with the directional flow of the organisation. We will come back to this key insight in Chapter 2, when we look at leadership.

Responsible leadership involves understanding the impact your behaviour has on others. This maybe through direct influence or by the decisions you make that may affect others indirectly. Healing organisations encourage this aspect of responsible leadership at every level in the organisation, but it will not happen unless it is positively modelled from the top.

Knowing yourself will require a continuous journey of self-discovery as we change with learning and experience. It is a worthwhile investment to explore the various psychometric tests available to you in order to explore the many dimensions of 'you' – your personality, your preferences, your strengths and areas for personal improvement. Tests are only useful if the feedback is given meaning, directed to the questions individuals have about themselves, and in this context, what the organisation demands or needs.

> **2. Align a sense of purpose for individuals, teams and the organisation.**

I have worked with many charismatic leaders, yet charisma, defined as 'the ability to make a lasting impression by their personality and manner', is no substitute for respecting the worth and value of others who work for you. Many leaders are unable to cope with the trappings and status of power and feel they have to live up to an image they believe is expected, yet they are often blind to what most people think of them. Therefore it's important to act with respect and sensitivity if the leaders want loyalty and commitment.

Act with respect and sensitivity

I believe there are four major spheres of respect and sensitivity that, when congruent in an individual, will create a sense of real direction, value and purpose. Gaining this congruence throughout an organisation will engender health, wellbeing and wealth for all.

Sphere 1 – Self-respect and sensitivity

Anyone in a leadership capacity models the behaviour that gets rewarded (i.e. many people will look up to them and take their cues for what's needed to be successful). If, as a leader, you work long hours and, in doing so, put your health and family life at risk, then this is not self-respect or sensitivity and may inadvertently be communicating to all your staff – 'this is what you expect them to be doing also'. This 'work hard' philosophy is sometimes accompanied by play hard mentality also. This then leads to behaviour and social activities conducted in the sense of 'I deserve it', 'let's have fun'. Unfortunately, these pursuits of pleasure are often designed to damage further the mental and physical sense of who we are by drinking too much and not getting enough healthy sleep. All of this could be interpreted as a lack of sensitivity to what you really need, and a lack of self-respect in terms of looking after yourself.

Understanding your own personal drivers and how they play out in your career decisions is important. Finding alignment between personal direction and organisation direction will increase the likelihood of life enhancing work.

Being healthy in mind, body and spirit is a prerequisite to self-respect and sensitivity. This will enable you to build on the next sphere with real integrity.

Sphere 2 – Respect and sensitivity for your staff

First of all, it is important to respect the fact that your staff have a life outside the workplace and have many talents other than those they bring to work. Respect the fact that they all have personal ambition and, given a chance, want to fulfil these ambitions or, at least, be recognised for doing a good job. If you demonstrate this respect by creating a working environment where they are encouraged to thrive and learn – then leadership at every level in the organisation is possible. This is manifested by individuals and teams taking personal initiatives to improve their own work situation (in doing so, they will feel more in control, increase the productivity levels and the enjoyment factor).

Sensitivity is expressed ideally by everyone in the organisation. This is sensitivity about the impact people have on each other, and the importance of recognising the internal interdependencies everyone has on each other. Creating an internal customer/supplier ethos can clarify these interdependencies and encourage the "give and take" negotiations that are such an important part of developing departmental functions into a corporate unified body, with a sense of collective identity.

Modelling of this sensitivity by senior managers is critical. Increasingly, the ability to express empathy is seen as a critical core competency for successful leadership.

Expressing this intelligence, empathy and sensitivity in a recruitment policy and the general approach to staff wellbeing (i.e. in fairness and non prejudicial treatment of staff) are all important realities of a sensitive and respectful organisation.

My way into corporate business life in the mid 80s began by sending a letter to five major companies with the hypothesis that "most senior managers in large organisations are at best deluded, at worse psychotic", as it is highly unlikely that they have real insight as to the impact their decisions or behaviour is having on the many thousands of people working for them. Curiously, this letter got me several interviews, one of which was successful and launched my transition from teaching psychiatry and psychology to organisation development!

Perhaps today senior managers are more savvy about the impact of their decisions and behaviour?

Sphere 3 – Respect and sensitivity for your customers and suppliers

Knowing your customer and the market, and being sensitive to changing trends and expectations, will help decisions about shifting resources and improving service. This respect can be reinforced by helping everyone in the organisation to recognise the importance of the customer/consumer – in that the measure of success has to be customer satisfaction through the optimum (i.e. most efficient) deployment of resources.

Customer-focused organisations are those that immediately show respect and sensitivity when designing the customer experience – from first contact to realisation of the product or service – if the customer is delighted then loyalty and word-of-mouth referrals create a critical mass of positive reputation, and hence the brand becomes synonymous with quality, value and care. Staying close to the customer and how they are thinking and responding to your service/product is a sign of respect that will reap rewards. If this feedback and intelligence is then channelled towards improvement and appropriate redesigns, then this will become evident by a growing and loyal customer following. Use of surveys, customer focus groups, learning from complaints and bringing customers into your training and development events can help reinforce the importance of the centrality of the customer.

Suppliers are often undervalued and taken for granted. Mismanagement of suppliers can result in significant business loss and customer dissatisfaction. Respecting what the supplier can offer, investing in them to help them align their strengths with what the company needs and involving them in discussions about company direction, can all contribute to an ethos of partnership, which in the long run will improve quality of supply and increase the likelihood of the supplier delivering beyond the ordinary!

Rather than beat them down to the bottom price and paying them late – better to select suppliers on the values they hold and their potential to grow with you. Enhance your reputation and theirs by encouraging consistency between their ethos of customer service and your own.

Sphere 4 – The community

What legacy will you leave the organisation when you leave? Many who work for years in one organisation become cynical of the ever-changing influx and departure of career-hungry managers. It is unfortunate that these people, and indeed the vast majority of managers enhancing their careers by moving onwards and usually upwards, interpret this movement as selfish. The bigger picture, however, can be exciting if, in today's world, the importance of leaving a legacy of improvement, be it customer experience, staff welfare, or eco-friendly policies, can be realised. The practice then of the rotation of leadership can be globally beneficial. To realise this, of course, one would have to see beyond the job and recognise it as an opportunity to make a positive difference, and contribute to wellbeing beyond the demands of the customer and staff.

Every organisation significantly impacts its immediate neighbourhood. Most organisations have a countrywide effect on people's lives in some way. Many have a global reach spanning many countries and continents. To what extent do companies debate and create opportunities to ensure their footprint is positive and enhancing the lives of others? Why should they do this? It may cost the company money. It may divert the company from its main purpose. The reason is both simple and powerful. By giving and putting back into the world system, the chance of a sustainable network of mutually enhancing relations begins to develop – increasing the chances of loyalty and longevity for the company and the planet!

For a company to have healing qualities that sustain itself and all its dependants, then the values of sensitivity and respect need to be more than words. These values need to be reflected in behaviour appropriate to the situation and the choices made.

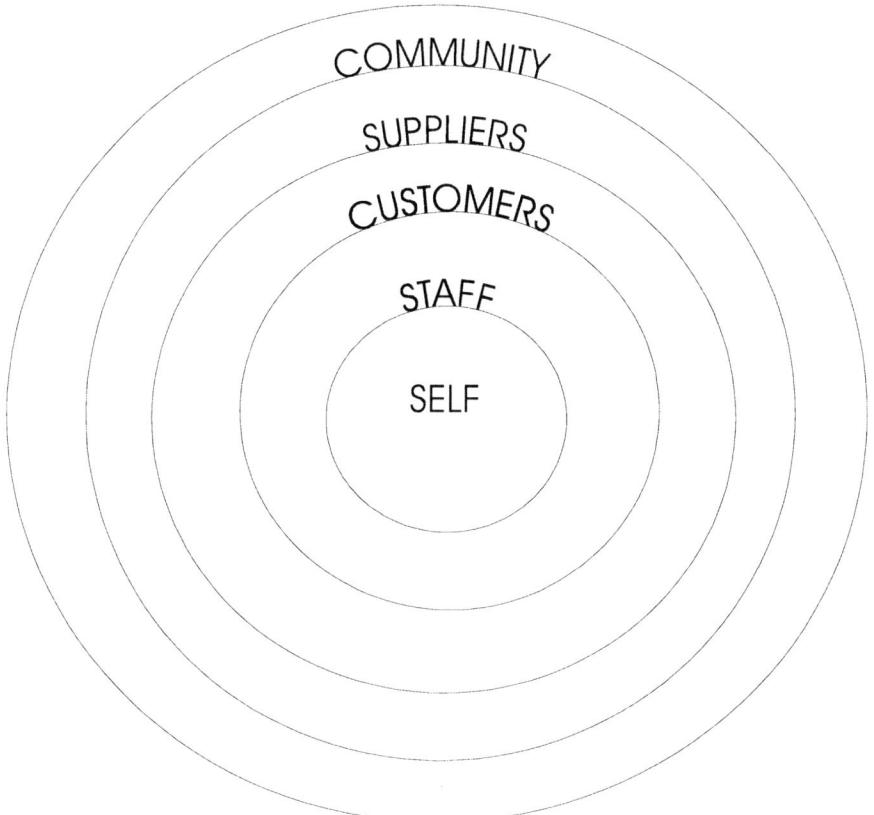

Figure 1. Aligning the values of respect and sensitivity

---

3. Create an ethos of respect and sensitivity to yourself, staff, customers, suppliers and the community.

Realise the power of choice

The more we are aware of how our emotions, attitudes and thoughts influence our behaviour, the more choices we have in terms of how to react to people and situations. If we take on the identity of a leader, whether as head of an organisation, department, team or just someone taking an initiative to influence or change something, then along with this role comes responsibility. The responsibility of having knowledge and control of what we are doing, combined with an insight as to the impact we are having on others, is a powerful combination. Focusing this power appropriately on the issues that matter can make the difference between staff that are in chaos and staff who feel reassured in that there is a direction and a sense of purpose.

Leading a process of Organisational Healing requires insightful positive thinking. Not blind optimism but a real sense of confidence in the potential of your team – i.e. given the right environment they can achieve extraordinary things. It's important to discard self-defeating beliefs and reinforce the alignment between your personal values and the organisational values. If there is a mismatch between these, then this will eventually create personal dissonance and the inevitable stress will create disease. For example, I worked with a firm of solicitors and helped them build a team and to reinforce the importance of customer service. They espoused the values of respect, honesty, integrity and sensitivity to the needs of clients/customers. However, their style of operating with each other was less than honest and far from sensitive. It became increasingly difficult to keep the values alive when dealing with the public when behind the scenes the atmosphere was very unhealthy. Eventually something had to break and formal complaints of harassment and mismanagement heralded a sad period of readjustment for this particular firm.

The leader in the case above was sufficiently open to the possibility that he may inadvertently, through his ambition and passion to grow the law firm, have put too much pressure on getting business, which resulted in stress and mistakes. However, he did recognise the power of review and feedback, i.e. if this is done at the service of learning and improvement, then mistakes and setbacks are not failures, just opportunities to get stronger and wiser. This then increases the chance of acting and not reacting, becoming solution-oriented rather than problem-bound, and open to learning new and smarter ways of working with renewed energy and enthusiasm, on the journey towards the optimum healthy organisation.

Be open

The quality of 'openness' is an important element in the continual journey of awareness. There is rarely a workshop or team event I run where the participants, when asked what ground rules they want to create for themselves, say 'openness'. Sounds fine in principle, but what does this mean? It can result in an insightful and robust discussion if you choose to elaborate. Here are some of the elements of openness explored through discussion in recent workshops

Open to learning

Using well known phrases or quotes from a variety of sources can be useful to get the debate going, for example:

> *'Minds, like Parachutes, work better when they are open.'*

> *'If you always do what you have always done you will always get what you have always got!'*

So, what encourages openness to learning? A non-judgemental and supportive atmosphere and trust. A willingness to take risks and make mistakes – sometimes a leap of faith to try something new. So, creating an open learning environment is far from straightforward and may require a little personal courage.

Being open – willing to disclose honestly one's views and opinions. One's feelings and reactions. To do this freely requires a degree of confidence that, when personal views are expressed, will not be judged or ridiculed.

Open to the opinion of others – perhaps accepting that your view is not the only view, and perhaps not appropriate at this time. To understand that there are differences in how people view the world and each other. People also have different ways of communicating and influencing, depending on their personality and culture. Respecting and learning from these differences is another form of openness.

Open – accessible, inviting and inclusive. It's amazing how intimidating a Board or executive team can be. They invariably underestimate the fear and anxiety created when an individual is asked to present or attend a well established and powerful team. How you reduce this fear and change your reputation around from it being an ordeal to it being an opportunity for recognition will, to a large extent, depend on how the qualities of openness are genuinely expressed through behaviour and communication.

Open Communication – This involves two-way communication, where there is a genuine attempt to encourage understanding of the message given and freedom is created to give messages back, about the impact and implications of any proposed changes. Many organisations have briefing mechanisms and *claim* the system is two-way, yet few manage to make it fully participative, and in reality there are usually only a few questions. The key here is to design these briefing sessions creatively, to encourage the staff to speak out and contribute.

The Johari window (See Figure 2) summarises the key ingredients that can encourage openness and, at the same time, makes a point that everyone has their limitations and boundaries. These boundaries need to be respected, and therefore the balance of feedback and disclosure is best maintained within the context of a personal contract. To do this one needs to establish the purpose of feedback and ensure it's based on the desires and wishes of the recipient. Following this understanding, and as long as the feedback is given with best intentions and is constructive – i.e. based on behaviour that can be changed – then the chance of the individual learning something new about themselves is increased. So, the arena is enlarged further, and perhaps the blind spot is reduced. This principle of encouraging openness can be applied at an individual, team, departmental or organisational level. It depends on the quality of data, information and willingness of the recipients to listen to the feedback. The more aware one is of what's going on, the more chance of making the right choices. Awareness is enhanced by increasing the possibilities for the quality of openness being realised at all levels in the organisation. This is aided by having a balance between honest disclosure and good quality feedback.

The Johari window, originally described by Joseph Luft and Harry Ingham in 1955[1], can be a useful framework for reviewing the quality of openness in any group or organisation.

> **4. Encourage the quality of meaningful openness at every level in the organisation.**

---

[1] Ingham, H. & Luft, J., 'The Johari Window: A Graphic Model of Interpersonal Awareness', *Proceedings of the Western Training Laboratory in Group Development*, Los Angeles: UCLA, 1955

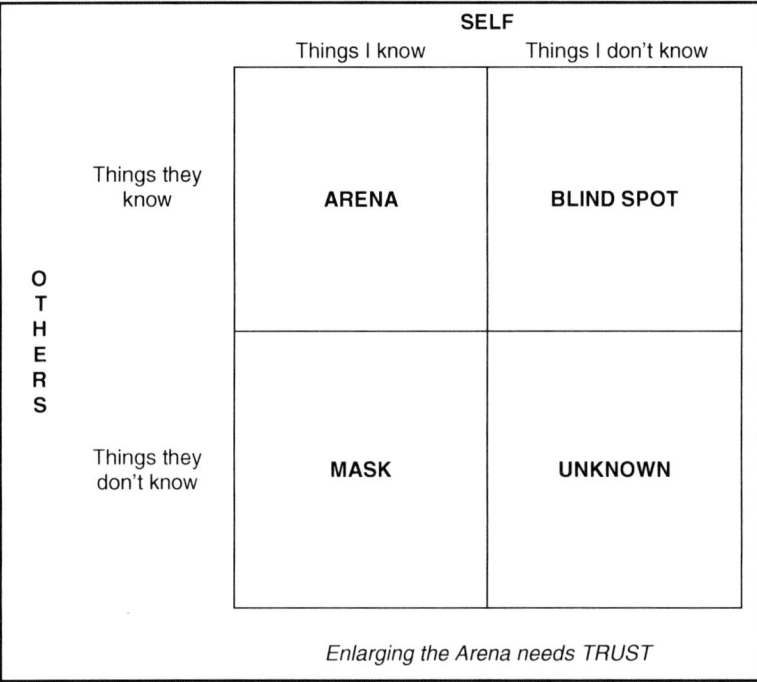

Figure 2. The Johari Window

The Johari Window has four "panes". It is based on the principle that of all the things about ourselves that exist to know:

1. *Some things will be known to ourselves and to other people.* This is shared knowledge and is the basis for all of our mutual dealings with one another. Usually called the "Arena", effective communication is enhanced when we work at maximising the size of this pane.

2. *Some things will be known to us but not to the people we deal with.* Called the "Mask" or the "Facade", this is the pane which encourages us to engage in games-playing, trickery, and defensiveness. The larger this pane, the less chance we have of developing truly meaningful and open relationships with others.

3. *Some things will be known to others but not to ourselves.* This is the "blind spot". This is potentially self-limiting to us because we risk exposing

ourselves to weaknesses which we don't know about and which can be exploited by others.

4. *Some things will be unknown to anyone* – ourselves and other people. This is the great "unknown". This is a potential source of personal creativity and other resources which we may never have realised existed.

Some individuals and organisations deliberately enter the unknown and are prepared to deal with the uncertainty involved. They recognise the need to balance opportunity with risk and, in doing so, often discover creative options for learning and growth.

The way to increase the size of the Arena, while decreasing the size of the other panes is first through self-disclosure (sharing information about the real you with others and thus increasing their knowledge about you) and secondly through obtaining feedback (getting open and honest information about yourself from those who witness you and your performance at work and elsewhere).

The window panes' size will vary, depending on the degree of trust that exists in the group or organisation. The greater the degree of trust, the bigger the 'arena' and the greater the chance of learning.

Boundaries, however, still need respecting, and in reality there are times when a leader cannot be totally open about what is going on. There are circumstances, through commercial or privileged information, that will place a person in a situation where it becomes inappropriate to convey what they know – until the facts are widely known or a decision has got to a stage of maturity, where people can be informed. These judgements need to be made in light of the values of the organisation and with the best interest of the business goals. Commercially and politically sensitive information can be leaked prematurely, causing unnecessary anxiety and uncertainty. Having an open communication policy means a regular and up-to-date two-way communication process on issues, so that all concerned can have an opportunity to understand what's really going on at any given time.

Blocks to awareness include the personal sense of satisfaction gained from having one's own sense of self-importance reinforced through the acknowledgement of others. This may be praise, admiration and gratitude; but could also be subservience, sycophancy, blind 'followership', fear and dependency. I have seen many a Chief Executive or Director communicate their intention to be open and reasonable and approachable, while their behaviour, manner and decision-making convey an egotistical status-consciousness that often creates a sense of having an actor in charge, and no one really knowing who this person really is. These ego-dominated people are often, deep down, uncertain as to their own effectiveness and may lack the people skills to gain cooperation and commitment without the threat of dictatorship and power.

On the other hand I have seen leaders who gain respect and followership to the extent that you could believe their staff would willingly do absolutely anything for them because of the genuine expression of who they are, their values and their vulnerability. They are genuine, without the airs and graces of status, and therefore their position ceases to be a barrier, and they become a positive role model of how to become successful. Being a leader is about being vulnerable – vulnerable because it requires courage to make a stand and to communicate a vision and ambition, supported by behaviours consistent with making the vision a reality. All of this is very visible, and when the leader trips up – it's amazing how many photographers and journalists turn up to record the event. However, they are less enthused about the day-to-day positive attributes and actions a leader has to conduct to maintain confidence and credibility.

Open up the opportunity for leadership

Remember – a leader can be anyone in the organisation who shows initiative to change and improves an aspect of their work. This is influence and power and can be realised in places often least expected.

Some examples I have come across are:

- The head porter in a hospital facilitating medical secretaries in how to reorganise the way medical notes were stored.

- A domestic assistant, when observing that most patients on a ward were not drinking the water routinely given to them in jugs before every shift, decided to stop putting the jugs out and handed them a glass of water instead every time she went past their beds. When the nurse in charge became aware of this she made it policy for all staff to do the same. They measured the difference – patients' hydration improved, time and water was saved! It then became hospital policy to do the same. The routine of giving jugs of water out was redundant. In fact, it was estimated that a jug of water cost 13 pence, of which 11.5 pence was wasted. The beauty of this project was that it cut across professional boundaries, saved and redirected staff time and was initiated from the front line.

- A phlebotomist (taker of blood), facilitating the change in how blood specimens were collected and results delivered, reduced patient stay by several days.

- The kitchen worker who observed what was wasted after meals, and took it upon himself to ask the customers why it wasn't good enough to take home – resulting in the restaurant's now famous catch phrase – What's left is always good enough to take home!

- The IT support worker who, on his own initiative, took it upon himself to get out of the department and walk round the organisation to ask if anyone is having any problems one hour a day and he solved many easy IT problems at a PC level – he got the reputation of being a super hero – this changed the perception and practice of the IT dept.

Awareness and belief of one's true potential can transform a work place and a community. Sometimes all it needs is a spark of enthusiastic optimism and belief that a better way of working and living is possible if everyone can work together towards a common goal.

Creating positive awareness

A healing organisation is one where positivity is tangible. You can see it in the faces of every person working there. Every response is positive, nothing is a problem and anything is possible. So, where does this positive outlook come from? If you have a critical mass of people who genuinely believe in success and optimistically seek out opportunities for improvement in everything they do. This then will attract further positive attitudes and will result in success.

This positive outlook makes it possible to develop a 'recognition and praise' culture. So often in organisations, particularly care or social service companies, there is an expectation that people will give more than what they get paid for. This wealth of goodwill is then taken for granted until it comes to the next round of pay talks and the workers realise they are not getting recognition and therefore demand a just return for their work or else it's work-to-rule – i.e. goodwill is withdrawn.

Communicating a positive vision and highlighting the success in the organisation will eventually create a "feel good factor" – this in itself will create a sense of belief that success is possible for all. Even in bad times, when there is a business downturn for whatever reason (disease, fuel price increases, war, or stock market crash), if the message is consistent (i.e. we will get through this if we stick together and believe in survival, recovery and eventual success) then low morale and depression can be avoided.

I remember working for the Airline company Cathay Pacific Airways when

SARS, 9/11 and a dramatic rise in fuel prices hit. This almost broke the company. It was only the strong leadership, the consistent communication and positive messages that "this is a phase and the company will recover" that gave hope to all concerned. Even when a proportion of the staff had to take one in four weeks unpaid leave, the morale remained positive, and indeed, this airline came back quicker than most others and now remains one of the best in the world. It believes it will be the best, and it continues to win the top awards in the industry. The airline exudes positive attitude, and you get the distinct impression that any of their employees would go that extra mile to ensure the customer gets satisfaction.

Bowlee Park Community School is a primary school in one of the most deprived areas in Manchester, UK. From being one of the worst performing schools in the country, recently it achieved the highest awards for educational standards in the country. When I was asked to design a conference to merge the school with another, I walked around the school and quickly sensed the positive air, the respect for children and the children's respect for teachers: the sense of fun and pride was tangible. Where does this come from? In this case, initially from the leadership – the Head Teacher clearly approached the transformation of the school with a belief that all the staff have great potential to pull together and make the school into a haven, an oasis for learning, where children could realise their full potential.

This positive belief, when communicated from a deep sense of conviction that achievement and realisation of the dream is possible, can create a sense of hope for everyone concerned. Positives attract and can become self-fulfilling.

Awareness is essential to enable personal effectiveness. To nurture a healing organisation you need to be a role model for healing yourself.

> **"Creativity, interpersonal effectiveness, the ability to 'contain' toxicity and help navigate through deep entrenched defences all are significantly enhanced by personal psychological and physiological health."**
> *Graham Barkus, Head of Organisation Development and Learning, Cathay Pacific Airways*

So, raising awareness of yourself, and realising the impact you make on those around you, creates an aura of responsible leadership and is the first element in creating organisational healing.

Raised awareness begins to model openness and creates the possibility for everyone to recognise their own contribution towards a positive vision of a healing organisation.

This raised awareness creates the opportunity for channelling the insights and realisation of potential to developing the skills and competencies of leadership at every level in the organisation. This is the focus for the next chapter, *Leadership – Channelling Personal Power.*

5. Ensure everyone understands the positive future picture that's possible to achieve.

2

Leadership – Channelling Personal Power

Harnessing personal power in a conscious and deliberate way is a fundamental element of responsible leadership. Doing this for the benefit of others creates the possibility of achieving sustainable improvement and long-lasting valued relationships. Misunderstanding your power or misusing it without thinking through the impact you have can create costly consequences.

Perhaps Dave Battle has had a chance to reflect a little about his style of operating.

Delectrex Limited

"OK, team – then that's agreed, we add openness, respect and sensitivity to our statement of values."

Dave Battle was feeling particularly smug with himself as he felt now he was winning the team over.

After a rocky start in his first few weeks he felt it was time for an open and honest discussion as to where he stood and what he expected from his team for the future. He realised that his initial attempt to make a positive impact had resulted in chaos and almost revolution. He needed to stand back, look at himself and the business and make the decisions in a more measured and inclusive way. Friday afternoon was dedicated to working together to agree a vision for the future and agree what Delectrex Limited – a medium-sized company supplying electrical systems and other tools and products to the motor trade – should focus on as priorities. Part of this exercise was also to spell out what values should drive staff behaviour, as Dave was very concerned about the low morale, the ongoing industrial unrest and some attitudes of his heads of department and supervisors.

"Have a good weekend everyone! Oh, Doreen, before you go, can I have a quick word."

Doreen Deli – the Marketing Director was usually full of life, a vivacious blonde with a big personality and well, big everything really!

"Doreen, you were a little quieter than usual today – are you OK with what I am proposing?" Dave was recalling his friend Ged's question about understanding one's own personal impact on others.

"Well to be honest, Dave, it sounds like you want to do my job!"

"I don't think so – what do you mean!"

"I am the one who usually decides which conferences we pitch at and when we run a sales conference for the whole team. You are introducing a new venue, suggesting a new market which has been tried before and failed, and the sales team have already got a date in the diary for this year for their team event."

"My dear Doreen," Dave moves closer and softens his tone – "I don't want to take over your job; these are only suggestions, good ones though, and if you want to give me good reasons for not going ahead then please let me know."

Normally, Doreen would flirt her way out of this situation, but the customary Friday afternoon gin and tonic with the team was now calling stronger than ever.

"OK, Dave I will send you an e-mail making my points clearer next week – must dash now – are you playing golf this week end?" Trying to change the subject!

"Oh yes – my usual round with my old friend Ged – you might have heard of him – quite a well-known management consultant."

"Er, no – must go – have a good one! Bye."

*   *   *   *   *

The Boardroom was silent and empty with its decoration of flip charts recording the team's aspirations and hopes for the future.

"Babs!"

"Yes, Mr Battle"

"Can you get these typed up and put them in a document form?"

"When do you need them?"

"ASAP"

"Now? I was hoping to get off. My grandchildren are staying this week end and . . . ."

"Fine! Don't worry, Monday morning will do. Have a good weekend." Dave also realised how fragile Babs was, so gently does it!!

*   *   *   *   *

"OK, Doreen, spill the beans. What did he want?"

"I need a drink first – a large gin and tonic please, Dan."

Somehow Dan always found himself getting in the first round – the reliable, over-conscientious Operations Director, still grieving over not getting the Managing Director's position.

Dan, Doreen, Dick the Finance Director and Daphne the Personnel Director have, over the past few years, made it a ritual to have a Friday afternoon catch-up in the local pub called The Grapevine in the nearby village. As yet no one has suggested inviting their new boss.

"I don't know why I bother," squawked Doreen. "He hasn't even read my Marketing plan – if he had, he surely wouldn't have suggested moving into the Tractor market and even going as far as suggesting what we should do at the next sales team conference!"

"That's nothing, Doreen," Dick McKavit spoke up. "He put brochures on my desk describing new accounts software – he hasn't got a clue about how the current system works and if he thinks my team could cope with a new system when they haven't got a hang of this one . . . .!"

"Oh come on, folks, he's not that bad," Daphne was always able to see the best in people. "You know, after a dodgy start he has at least spent the afternoon working with us to get a clearer sense of direction for the company."

"Bollocks!" shouted Doreen. "Most of the afternoon he spent telling us what he wants – and this rubbish about respect, openness and sensitivity – he's got as much sensitivity as I have got in my . . . ."

"Keep your voice down, he's just walked into the pub." They all looked round sheepishly and moved closer together, huddled in the dark recess of this old country pub.

"Oh shit, what do we say? Has he seen us?" Dick looked at Daphne. "Go on, you better go to him and invite him over."

"Too late."

"Aye up – what's this – a conspiracy meeting – not planning a mutiny are you?" Dave laughed, trying to hide his surprise and disappointment that his team should think of having a social drink without him.

"Oh no, nothing like that, it was just a spur of the moment thing really – come and join us. Can I get you a drink, Boss?" Dan in a sycophantic manner jumped up, offered Dave his seat and reached into his pocket yet again . . . .

*   *   *   *   *

"You know – I am going to say something when we go into the club."

"Oh, come off it, Dave – it's not that bad, after all we are in a competition."

"Look, a three-ball – whether in a competition or not should finish in under four hours for God's sake, and if you look at how long they are taking to putt – bloody ridiculous!"

Ged was ready for Dave's customary rant about something, which usually was a sign that he was ready to talk about work.

"Why is everything so bloody slow? Even my team at work seem to be on some form of tranquilizer!"

"I thought you didn't want to talk about work on the course?"

"Well, it's the last hole and if I wait any longer . . . ."

"You're doing OK – you're ahead on points – you only have to par this and you beat me for a change."

"Ha! Well – it's just that every bit of advice I give the team they just don't appreciate it and they are reluctant to act on it – I don't think they are giving me the respect I deserve."

"Giving advice, huh?"

"What's wrong with that?"

"Let's talk further when we get in – it's your honour."

Dave lined up – took his usual aggressive warm-up practice swing, wriggled his wrist and . . . .

"I wouldn't if I were you, Dave."

"What!!!?" Dave stood back. "What are you on about, Ged – I was just about to hit."

"Well, you were lining up and aiming well out of bounds to the right – now unless you can hook the ball deliberately, which I doubt because you usually slice it, then I would hate for you to have a bad last hole and lose the game. If I were you I would aim to the left towards the wood."

"Ok – thanks, Ged."

Dave readjusted – two even more aggressive practice swipes, a wriggle of the wrist and . . . . .

"Oh for God's sake – that's ridiculous – that's your fault, Ged – I've probably lost the bloody thing in the woods now – so much for your advice."

"Exactly," said Ged with a smile "let's forget that one, have another shot . . . ."

In this Chapter, we explore what it takes to develop a style of leadership that creates effective problem-solving, team work, empowerment and delegation. Mainly:

- Styles of leadership.
- The process of empowerment.
- Force field analysis.
- The leader as a coach.
- Trust and delegation.

Styles of leadership

There are many different styles of leadership and the most effective leaders are able to adapt their style appropriately, depending on the demands of any given situation. It seems that our Mr Battle has but one style – rather directive and based on his perception that he knows best. The time where this is appropriate is when a specialist or expert is leading on a particular project or initiative that is dependent on their expert input. A Managing Director or General Manager such as Mr Battle is rarely in this position and, therefore, needs to adapt to a style of operating that gets the best out of the people he or she has, rather than suppressing the team's contribution through imposition of what may be naïve or inappropriate suggestions, from a position of status or power. Good intentions, but a trap that many people new to a job fall into – they feel they have to make a tangible contribution by offering new ideas or new ways of working. The alternative is to learn from what's working well, build on this and then encourage others to find ways of improving what's not working so well.

Of course, any new person will bring fresh views and new ways of looking at things – the way this can be expressed is through timely questions and involving others in a discussion about alternative ways of working.

The following is an outline of different approaches to leadership. Before you read this it may be interesting to complete the following questionnaire – even better if you dare – get your team to complete it, rating you as a leader then compare your self-perception with the perception your team have of you. (For a discussion of the interpersonal skills of effective leaders see also page 166).

The following questionnaire is taken from my book *54 Approaches to Managing Change at Work.*

Questionnaire

On a scale of 1 to 5, (1 being strongly disagree and 5 being strongly agree) rate your responses to the following statements:

1. I am seen as very approachable by my staff.

2. They perceive me as a good listener.

3. They learn a considerable amount from me by the way I manage the business.

4. They recognise me as one who will accept them and understand them as a person as well as a work unit.

5. We review regularly our meetings, strategy and the direction we are going.

6. There are very few non-discussible issues in our team meetings.

7. I welcome feedback about my performance, management style and decision-making and people management abilities from my people.

8. My team know exactly where they stand in terms of what I think of them in relation to their ability, performance and potential.

9. My team and I understand and are aware of the impact of our behaviour on shaping organisational values, attitudes, and hence performance.

10. I challenge myself on the assumptions and judgements I hold, particularly those that are likely to influence major decisions.

Add your score up.

If you score top marks, **35 – 50**, congratulations! You are either living out of leadership values or you are kidding yourself in terms of how you really are seen. I would advise you to definitely check out your self-perception with the perception of your staff; that is – get them to fill in the same questionnaire focused on you.

If you scored between **25 – 35**, you have some room for improvement, your strengths and weaknesses are probably known to you and you are probably attempting to be seen to be open to personal change and development. It would be important for you to build on success and, in some pragmatic way, demonstrate your change.

If you have scored in the lowest bracket, **0 – 25**, then you either need some help, or you do not recognise the value of this particular style of working or you are underestimating your performance in these areas.

Whatever your score on these questionnaires it will do you no harm to learn more about yourself, how you are seen by others and recognise that there is always choices about how you react and conduct yourself in order to positively influence any given situation.

Situational leadership

A good leader will find they adopt a style to suit the current situation. For example, in a crisis or emergency; this requires quick and directive decision-making skills, however, to achieve a task dependant on several people's contributions, requires a more democratic, delegating/team style of leadership.

A good leader will assess the situation and decide on the basis of:

- Skill levels and experience of the team – the balance between getting the job done in the short term and the opportunity for coaching and self-sufficiency in the longer term.
- The work involved (complex, team development, creative, routine).
- Organisation or business environment (e.g. competitive, changing, at risk or under threat).
- Their own strengths and natural/preferred style of working.

Leadership styles will vary depending upon the degree of supportive and directive behaviours. This can be summarised in the diagram set out in Figure 3, adapted from the work of Hersey and Blanchard (1982).

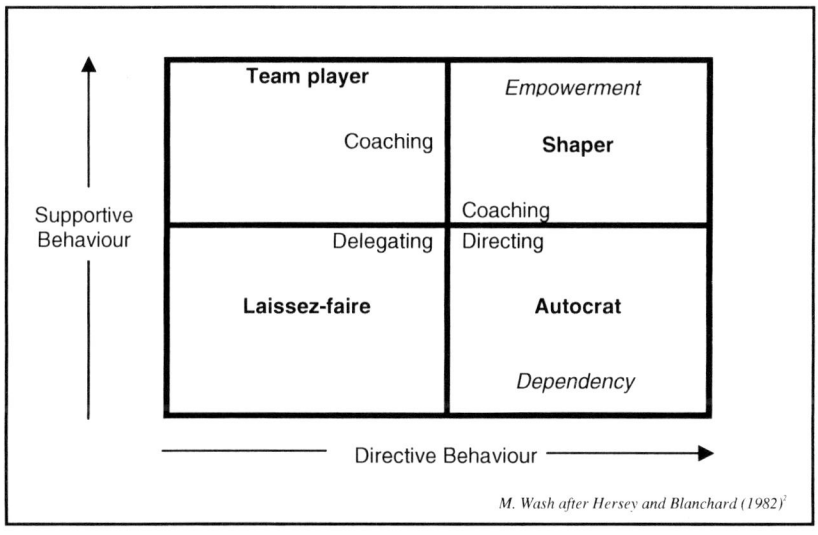

Figure 3

6. **Make leadership, its meaning, style and development a priority for the business.**

---

[2] Hersey, P. & Blanchard, K., *Management of Organisation Behaviour*, Prentice Hall, 1982

There are many ways of describing leadership styles. Some of the more popular ones are:

Autocratic

High control and high power. Often conveyed by strong egos who have little time for 'bottom-up' feedback! Can create a dependent, fearful and resentful workforce. Rarely seen as effective in today's highly modernised and expectant workforce society.

Transactional leadership

A leader who works through clear structures, has clarity about what they require of subordinates and relies heavily on reward and discipline as a way of control. Strong management with clear contracting regards expectations. Tends towards the autocratic approach.

Bureaucratic

Standards, procedures, audit, quality control, laws, rules, regulations, policies and hierarchy. These are the elements of most organisations. Always appropriate, especially where safety and complex law or finance is involved, but not as a substitute for creativity, imagination and drive. They are essential aspects of governance. However, when they become the main drivers of behaviour and cease to serve the business, then much waste can be associated with bureaucracy.

Charismatic

Highly motivating, full of enthusiasm. Often the personality behind a brand which can have value in its own right. Charismatic leaders sometimes run the risk of putting their ego or self image first – taking their eye off the ball, or neglecting the basics of organisation performance.

Democratic

The listening leader. Decision-making by majority or consensus. Involves others which enhances motivation and satisfaction. Can involve slow consultative procedures but the end result is often more acceptable than being dictated to.

Laissez-faire

Only works when you have a very self-sufficient team and you provide a strategic overview and monitoring role. Can be too 'laid-back' or 'let go' too much – thus resulting in a team lacking direction.

Task-oriented versus people-orientated leadership

Extreme task leaders will drive to get the job done, no matter what the cost. Often neglecting or blind to the stress and wellbeing of the staff. The people-orientated leader will work through the feelings and needs of team members with consideration of their talents and wellbeing. The extreme people-orientated leader may run the risk of missing deadlines.

In reality, leaders need a balance of both qualities.

Servant leadership

These people may not have positional leadership, but are seen as influential on the basis that they just quietly and successfully get on with the job. They create a followership based on their successful and enthusiastic approach. They also may have 'sapiential authority', i.e. instructing or directing out of expertise and not out of structural or positional authority.

Transformational leadership

Inspires others, through the communication of a vision, which binds everyone together. Explicit values are expressed and the performance of behaviours which are consistent with organisational values are rewarded.

These leaders are highly visible and put a great emphasis on the importance of communication.

Effective transformational leaders build teams around them, ensuring visionary strategy is translated into pragmatic goals and in turn, are followed through with importance placed on feedback and learning. This is summarised in Figure 4 below.

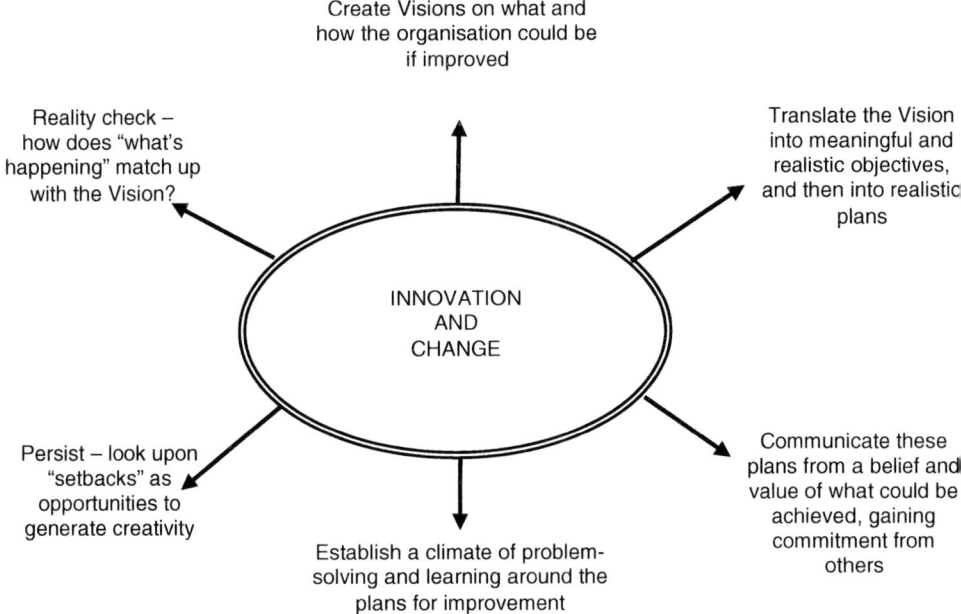

Figure 4. Transformational leadership process

Consider the following:

- What style of leader are you?
- What style of leader is needed in your job/organisation?
- What style of leader do you want to be?

The above summary of leadership styles was adapted from my book *54 Tools and Techniques for Business Excellence*.

The process of empowerment

Whatever style of leadership is adopted the end result needs to relate to improve performance and quality of experience for all concerned. This requires a sense of belief that, given the opportunity, individuals will thrive and achieve extraordinary things. This belief alone, however, is not enough. It needs expressing, with skill and awareness and the right questions, in order to know when it's appropriate to let go and trust, and when there is a need to coach and perhaps at times offer information to enable others to make a more informed choice.

Many competent individuals find themselves in management/leadership positions because they have been effective at solving problems and managing change within their previous sphere of control. They were considered experts in their own specialist area, and created a dependency around them. This can be recognised and interpreted as criteria for promotion. However, the successful individual eventually realizes that the style of operating in their previous position does not necessarily work as well in a position with greater responsibility and wider sphere of influence. As in Dave Battle's case, he thinks the best way to manage is to give his team his ideas and suggestions as to how to improve things, as opposed to enabling them to come up with solutions themselves. Managers like this need an alternative to solving everyone else's problems in order to show their team the best way of managing, or else they will find they are leading a suppressed and dependant team, and working all hours just to keep afloat. The alternative is the successful application of a coaching model that enables others to solve their own problems and to take ownership of change.

This approach can be achieved if the person influencing (i.e. the leader) understands how optimum change and improvement is created by the application of good questions, skills and techniques within a coaching framework to help individuals solve their own problems, and initiate the improvements they have some control over.

---

7. Learn how to enable others to lead.

A framework that enables this is Gerard Egan's Model B, as described in his book, *The Skilled Helper, A Systematic Approach to Effective Helping*[3]. See Figure 5 on page 50.

However, it is a rare event to see this process practised effectively as most people resort to a two stage problem-solving process, i.e. now I know what the problem is, I know what to do about it, instead of pausing and asking – now we know what the problem is what, ideally, do we want? What's the outcome we are looking for? What's the goal? Once these are set then the actions can be more appropriately aligned to ensure the goals are achieved. More importantly, the central component of the process is potentially the most creative. Here individuals

---

[3] Egan, G., *The Skilled Helper – A Problem Management Approach to Helping*, 6th ed, Brooks Cole, 1998

and teams can be given the permission to dream, to create the ideal picture out of which can come a real sense of direction and commitment to achieve together what's possible for a better future.

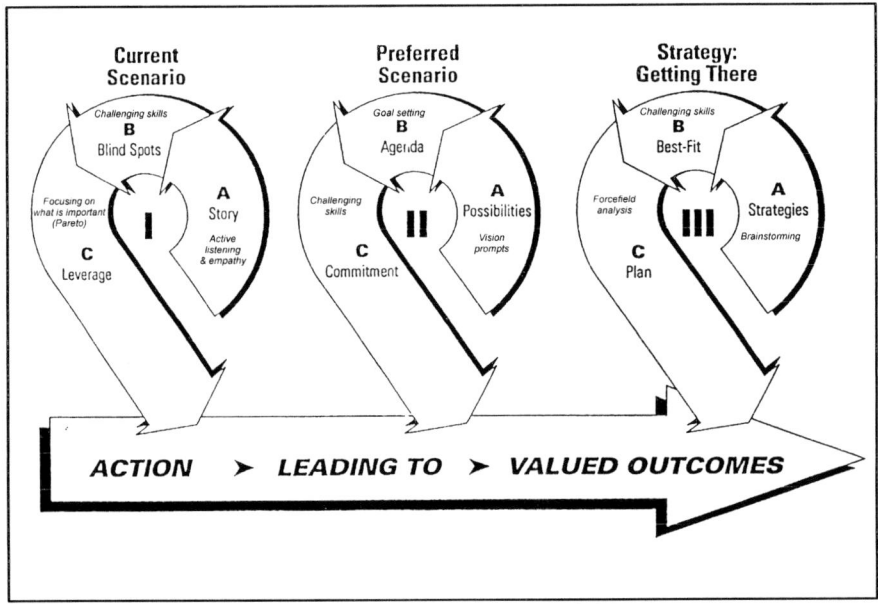

Figure 5. Gerard Egan's Model B

To encourage the practice of more effective change management, the manager/leader must model the process. This essentially means applying the following 9 steps:

1. Manage by fact (Model B, refer to 'A: Story')

A Healing Organisation is one where there is free flow of open and honest dialogue of what's going on. The challenge is to create an environment where people feel free to speak up without fear. Many of the world's disasters have been as a direct consequence of people not challenging, as a result of fear. The Challenger Disaster, with catastrophic loss of life, could have been avoided if the fault in the O ring had been discussed more openly, and the powers that be had encouraged the feedback and listened. The Piper Alpha oil rig blast in the North Sea – burning and killing dozens of men, may have been avoided if the relationship between management and staff unions, and the communication between shifts were more open and less adversarial. The importance of creating a listening organisation cannot be underestimated. If there is a blame culture then mistakes will be hidden, and sometimes those mistakes can have serious consequences.

Management by fact means reducing the level of inference – i.e. minimize gossip and rumour by regular communication and the open gathering of robust and reliable data. Once a problem or opportunity for improvement has been identified then getting close to the source of the issue needs to happen by good questioning, a focused survey and the collection of intelligence and data from different perspectives. Without good information, people will naturally escalate up to a level of inference that means management by assumption, rather than fact. This can be so wrong, with a consequence of going down an inappropriate path of change resulting in inefficiency and waste. (See page 200.)

2. Find out what's really going on (Model B, refer to 'B: Blind Spots')

Gathering the information and getting the facts may however not be enough. Sometimes you may have to dig deeper by asking what's really going on. Organisations, and indeed individuals, will have blind spots, i.e. they may be too close to the situation to see what's going on clearly. Therefore, they may need help to see clearly what are often difficult issues. These issues may be related to management style, bullying, sexual harassment, fraud, theft and other issues that are difficult to admit may go on in your organisation. The healing process must involve the honest recognition that all may not be well, and hiding the issues in the shadows will only run the risk of normalizing or institutionalising substandard behaviors and processes. (Refer to Chapter 7, Cure, page 180.)

The question to ask – "How has this happened?" – needs to be asked without blame, in a constructive way and with the intention to learn. For real insight and learning to take place, however, the question needs to go further – to ask "How did we get into this situation in the first place? What events led up to us creating this problem, situation or inefficient low quality product/service?" (Refer to double-loop learning, page 201.)

Using techniques like cause and effect analysis and 'why, why, why' (*54 Tools and Techniques for Business Excellence,* Technique N° 1, page 15 and N° 8, page 38) can help a group or team share their perceptions and experiences of what's really going on.

A critical aspect of finding out what is really going on is to clarify who is actually accountable for the change or intended improvement. Whatever is proposed needs to have clarity as to who is going to be effected and who is in control and responsible for the change. Discovering what your true sphere of control is can be empowering, in that you can quickly realise that a lot of wasted emotional energy can be spent on issues or situations not within your control.

> **8. Make the 'process of empowerment' a core competency for all managers.**

3. Focus on what's important (Model B, refer to 'C: Leverage')

When gathering information about any situation the danger is to create a level of complexity that stops the wood being seen because the trees get in the way! It's important to have criteria to cut down the amount of information and identify the core issues. Having good and meaningful data/information on an ongoing basis can help the process of problem identification be more efficient.

Pareto's well-known 80:20 rule applies here – 20% of information gathered will describe 80% of the problem. So let's identify the important elements and focus on the issues we can do something about (i.e. within our sphere of influence).

A mistake that some managers use in the data-gathering stage is to become too pedantic about the detailed statistics and measures. The validity of the information needs to be confirmed but not at the expense of days and sometimes weeks gathering more information that will not fundamentally alter the core issue being recognized. Moving on without the full picture need not be a problem, as long as the data gathered so far is appropriately interpreted, and further information about the situation may be gathered throughout the process of improvement.

4. Create a vision of what's possible (Model B, refer to 'A: Possibilities')

This is the central and most creative part of the process. It should be positive and uplifting because it involves describing the ideal picture. Using **vision prompts** to ask the questions:

- What would the situation look like if it was ideal?
- Who would be involved?
- Where would this take place?

- What would be in place?
- How would people be feeling?
- What would your reputation be?
- What would staff, customers, suppliers and the community be saying about you?
- What systems, policies and processes would ideally be in place to support the situation?
- What business results/outcomes will be evident?

Asking these questions can make a significant difference to an individual or team who wish to improve their situation. If only Mr Battle had asked his Finance Director – Dick, if, in an ideal world, the finance system was working to his satisfaction what would it look like? Rather than placing software brochures on his desk. Or to Doreen the Marketing Director – What would an increase in market share or the ideal market projection for our product look like? It's clear from the review of the workshop his team did not experience these Vision prompt questions when agreeing the company direction, therefore; their commitment to the work and decisions made so far may not be strong.

5. Set SMARTER goals (Model B, refer to 'B: Agenda')

From what may be a very colourful and positive picture now needs to come the reality of goal setting.

The bridging question from the Vision to Goals is:

Out of this vision what makes sense for us to achieve – what will make the most significant impact towards us achieving the vision described?

Choosing several key goals at this stage is important. Also, to recognise the difference between goal and action. The goal needs to be stated in outcome terms. It is important not to confuse 'ends' with 'means'.

For example the following is *not* a goal:

'By the end of next year we will have eight more sales people in the team.'

This is an action. The test question in this case would be: What would eight sales people give you? What's the outcome you are wanting? The outcome is likely to be increased sales and increasing your sales team is only one of many ways to do this.

So, once the goal statements are agreed you can use the mnemonic SMARTER to test out whether the goal will stand up to scrutiny:

S – Specific or Simple – is it clear to anyone reading it – does it refer to tangible things and minimises the chance for misinterpretation

M – Measurable – how will you know you have achieved it – what will be seen, evident, the impact it will make.

A – Appropriate – is the goal consistent and supportive of the company/organisation values, can it be tracked back to supporting strategic objectives.

R – Realistic – achievable – how confident are you in achieving it? It may be challenging but not too far-fetched to be potentially de-motivating.

T – Time framed – there is an indication of when the goal should be achieved.

The next two letters link to the next stage in the process – commitment.

E – Energy/enthusiasm – what level of motivation is there to achieve this goal?

R – Resources – both in terms of personal resources (i.e. willing to make time for this) and external resources (the support available). Do the benefits exceed the cost?

6. Test out commitment (Model B, refer to 'C: Commitment')

Exploring the last two issues in goal-setting (enthusiasm and resources) will begin to give an indication of how much commitment there is to achieve the goal. Gaining an appreciation of commitment at this stage is important as it may uncover what previously may have been hidden objections, reservations or other reasons why the proposed change may be resisted.

Up till now within the process it has been important to encourage positive thinking and to avoid the "yes but....." syndrome. However, now it will be important to pick up the clues related to potential resistance and listen and empathise with the views. Working through these reservations at this stage will uncover more information related to the issue and it may be better to be prepared to revise the goal statement than to force through a goal that will cause problems later on.

It's important to ask why the achievement of the goal is important. What it's worth, who will benefit and what if we didn't go for it and did something else instead? The answer to these questions will give a clearer indication as to the level of commitment. Better still – it may make explicit the values underpinning the work planned and hence increase the degree of motivation, commitment and ownership, and therefore the likelihood of completion is increased.

Throughout this process the importance of helping the team take ownership of the change as opposed to the person in charge imposing the change is critical. The contrast between the dictator and the facilitator is clear here. The former imposes his or her own suggestions, the latter creates the opportunity for others to create their own change.

7. Encourage creative ideas and options as to how to achieve the goals (Model B, refer to 'A: Strategies')

Once goals have been agreed the opportunity to be creative reoccurs in the process of brainstorming the many ways of achieving the goal. So often when someone recognizes what the problem is, they not only jump straight to a solution, but choose the first or most obvious thing to do, which may not be the best. It makes sense, therefore, to spend time tapping into the creativity that exists in any individual or team, especially if they are given a chance to employ it.

Brainstorming – i.e. encouraging as many ideas as possible and recording these initially without judgment or discussion, and therefore listening and building on each other's ideas – can generate a rich list of possible actions and methods to engage in to support achievement of the goals set.

Sometimes using the following prompts can encourage a team or individual to go further in coming up with ideas for action:

- What things could help?
- Who could support this and how?
- What can you learn from others who have done this well?
- What systems or processes may help?
- What existing strengths in the team/organisation can be applied to this situation?
- What's the wildest, most ridiculous thing you can think of that we could do to achieve our goal?

This last prompt is aimed at giving the permission to be creative – think out of the box. So often, when this happens, the grains of something new can be discovered, and it just may be that this new idea makes the difference between achieving the goal successfully, and achieving it successfully with a competitive edge, i.e. ahead of the game, innovative enough to stand out from your competitors.

8. Choose the best ones (Model B, refer to 'B: Best Fit')

It's amazing how out of many brainstormed lists of new ideas, the ones chosen are often in the first three and the last three – the last three often being the innovative ideas that make a difference. So it goes to show, by not giving the opportunity for staff to release their views about different ways of working, you are suppressing the potential commitment, enthusiasm, motivation and goodwill related to implementing their own, often better ideas for improving their own work situation.

The more staff feel in control of their own sphere of responsibility, then the more chance of them stepping in to improve their own work situation with a greater sense of satisfaction. The more control a manager takes away from his/her staff, the more chance of creating dependency and dissatisfaction.

So, even at this stage, the choice of what methods to employ, needs to belong to those responsible for following through on the actions.

The questions to ask at this stage are: "Out of this list of possible actions/ideas, which are the ones we could realistically do? Which ones, if achieved will make a significant difference? Which ones involve least cost with most benefit? Which ones do we need to do first?"

The answer to these questions will begin to form a sequence of actions that are the makings of a plan for improvement.

9. Plan for success – detailed first steps, ownership and accountability (Model B, refer to 'C: Plan')

Most plans suffer from two syndromes:

- **Inertia.** They fail to even go past first base – they fail to get beyond the first step. This is usually because they haven't been thought through, in sufficient detail, what needs to be done to ensure the first step is successful, often underestimating the amount of planning and preparation needed.

- **Entropy.** Things fall apart shortly after they have started. Again, mainly because people do not think through or plan for the possible obstacles or challenges on the way and, therefore, when it becomes perceived as too difficult, the action is reduced to 'try again later' or 'too difficult, so let's change our plan' or 'we need to re-think the method used' – all of which are unlikely events.

A technique to help plan in the details for successful action, and to increase the readiness to tackle challenges, is force field analysis, described below.

Force field analysis

What is it?

Force field analysis is a tool for increasing the chances of successful actions and was first described by Kurt Lewin in 1947.[4] It enables identification of the forces that will help or obstruct the initiation or maintenance of the desired change.

Force field analysis is a problem-solving technique which enables forward planning. The identification and graphic representation of the forces which will have a positive helping effect, and those forces which will have a negative hindering effect enable assessment of the ease or difficulty which is likely to be encountered when implementing a desired change.

The underlying principle of force field analysis is *forewarned is forearmed!*

When to use it

When there is a perceived need for change or improvement, force field analysis can be used to:

1. Identify the positive forces which will help, and the negative forces which will hinder, the proposed change to improvement.
2. Assess the ease or difficulty of achieving the proposed change or improvement.
3. Plan how to overcome the barriers to the proposed change or improvement.

Key steps

1. Define the problem: what is the current situation.
2. Define the objective: what is the aim or goal?
3. Prepare the force field diagram.
4. Identify the positive forces and represent them on the force field diagram.
5. Identify the negative forces and represent them on the force field diagram.
6. Identify actions to *increase* the effect of the positive forces.
7. Identify actions to *reduce* the effect of the negative forces.
8. Identify those actions needed to take place.
9. Plan, in detail, what you are going to do and when you are going to do it.

See Figure 6.

---

[4] Lewin, K., *Field Theory in Social Science*, Harper & Row, NY, 1951

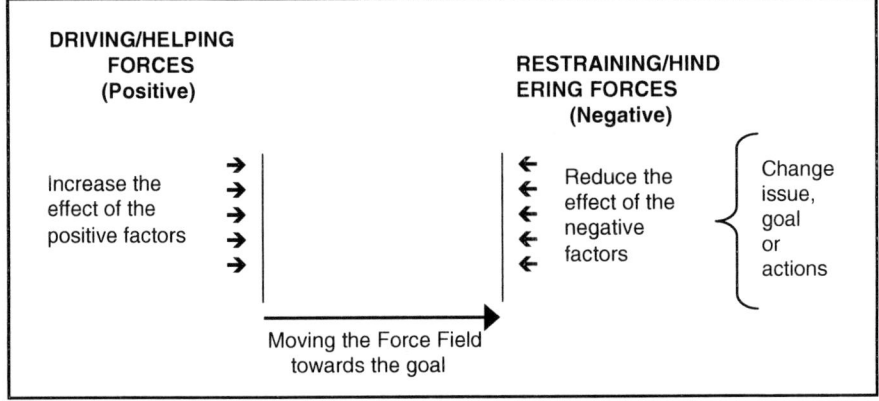

Figure 6. Force field analysis

By spending time on first steps, especially in a team situation, you will increase confidence and commitment to follow through.

From this early planning stage a more detailed and robust critical path of events can be detailed out. The quality of this planning will be significantly enhanced because of the previous work done in the previous stages, and the commitment gained from all concerned. This method of working is indicative of facilitative leadership and is not dependent on the expert input of the leader.

In summary, the process of empowerment goes beyond trust and delegation. It requires the timely and skilful application of questioning and other techniques within this 'coaching framework'.

> **9. Develop a shared language of managing change and problem-solving in the context of empowerment.**

The leader as a coach

Within a healing organisation this facilitative/coaching style of operating will be evident in key parts of the business. The process is particularly powerful for:

- Managing projects.
- Reviewing performance.
- Developing leaders.
- Reviewing progress.
- Strategic direction.

1. Project management

Each project will need to respect the phases of empowerment/problem-solving described above. Ideally, this methodology will be shared amongst all project leaders so a common language can develop and the exchange of progress for each project becomes easier through the question 'what stage are you at?' See page 150.

2. Personal performance/development review

A coaching style of reviewing each individual's progress in his or her current role will increase the likelihood of staff ownership of personal development. The conversation between boss and employee is likely to be much more productive and career-enhancing, if the coaching model is applied. For example:

- So how well do you think you are currently doing? (PRESENT)
- What do you want to achieve this year? (FUTURE)
- How many ways can you think of to achieve what you want? (ACTION)

This example is abbreviated but captures the message that asking and encouraging ownership of development will empower. The alternative of giving targets and suggesting how to go about achieving these will take the perception of control away from employees and run the risk of demotivating them.

3. Leadership development and training programmes

Integrating the skills and qualities required in facilitative leadership to the style of leadership development and related training programmes, will build up this coaching/facilitating approach as a core competency for the organisation.

4. Review of progress

General reviews of initiatives or progress can use the core questions associated with the approach i.e.

- To what extent have we progressed from the current situation? (PRESENT)

59

- How well have we achieved the goals? (FUTURE)
- What progress are we making with the implementation of the changes? (ACTION)

5. Strategic direction

- Do we know what's going on currently with our performance and how we compare with our competitors? (PRESENT)
- Are we clear as to our Vision and strategic Goals? (FUTURE)
- What progress are we making in achieving our Goals? (ACTION)

Underpinning all these opportunities to apply facilitative leadership is the value of learning. The willingness to encourage feedback as to the reality of progress – what's helping and hindering, and what we should pay attention to in order to increase our chances of success.

Trust and delegation

Trust is essential for an organisation to heal itself and thus sustain a long and healthy future. Trust encourages satisfaction, productivity and creates an open and responsive atmosphere.

The alternative to trust is suspicion and extreme auditing and policing of activity, which can undermine the confidence of all concerned.

Trust can be demonstrated in the way delegation is practised, the way individuals are left to get on with achieving their objectives, and the degree of risk-taking by leaders willing to encourage their staff to try new things.

In summary:

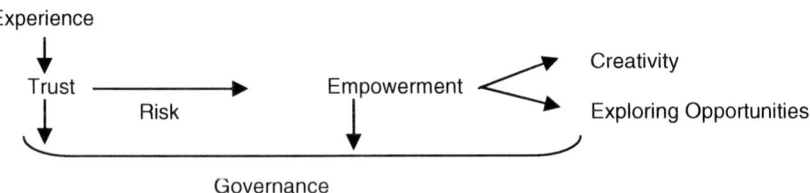

(acknowledging Professor Tom McGuffog)

60

Leaders have a responsibility to encourage trust at all levels in the organisation. Whether someone trusts people at work may relate to the beliefs and values about how people conduct themselves at work, and what they believe motivates people.

Leadership styles can be significantly influenced by the leaders' beliefs about the motives of their workforce. This was first described by Douglas McGregor (1960)[5] in his Theory X and Theory Y hypothesis:

Theory X assumptions are that:

1. Employees are inherently lazy and will avoid work unless forced to do it.
2. Employees have no ambition or desire for responsibility; instead they prefer to be directed and controlled.
3. Employees have no motivation to achieve organisational objectives.
4. Employees are motivated only by physiological and safety needs.

Theory Y assumptions are that:

1. Employees find work as natural as play if organisational conditions are appropriate.
2. Employees can be motivated by higher order needs such as ego, autonomy and self-actualisation.
3. Employees seek responsibility since it allows them to satisfy higher order needs.

Effective leaders tend to adopt Theory Y beliefs.

Those who adopt Theory X beliefs are likely to resort to control and policing methods to manage their staff – resulting in a suppressed and suspicious work culture. A healthy organisation is one where workers find work as natural as play, there is a strong alignment between a personal sense of purpose and the opportunity the organisation creates to enable that person to fulfill their purpose.

To shift from a non trusting environment to one where people feel valued and trusted is not always a smooth transition, as words need to be backed by deeds as the staff under a culture of suspicion are likely to have adopted the same viewpoint – i.e. suspicious and cynical. Change can be achieved over a sustained period of positive modeling from the senior managers who demonstrate through their behaviour that trust underpins how work is delegated and decisions are made.

More trust will lead to:

---

[5] McGregor, D. *The Human Side of Enterprise*, McGraw-Hill, 1960

- less secrecy
- less referral upwards
- less looking after self and watching one's own back
- less defensiveness
- less cliques and less internal competitiveness
- less burn-out of bosses who don't trust others to do the work so take it on themselves
- less 'it's more than my job's worth' i.e. inflexibility.

> **10. Encourage appropriate risk/opportunity management and a climate of learning and problem-solving through relationships based on trust. Clearly define your governance.**

Trust will develop between people if there is mutual respect, and this will increase through an increased knowledge of each other. Leaders who stay aloof may inadvertently create suspicion through lack of personal contact and lack of accessibility. Leaders need to be seen to be approachable and accessible and they need to demonstrate a genuine interest in the people that work for them – not just as workers but as people with interests outside of work and ambition and hopes for the future. Showing a real sense of interest and care will eventually create that sense of mutual trust, and therefore the traditional boss subordinate relationship becomes akin to a partnership, where there is 'a looking out for each other' mentality, and hence a win-win relationship.

Developing trust takes time and may initially seem risky, especially for all those managers who are used to being in control and having a 'hands on' view of the world, as in the case of our Mr Battle. To delegate appropriately, you need to recognize the capability of your staff and allocate with the right level of support. Building in a contract of support and review following task allocation, or explanation of responsibility, will ensure there are sufficient updates and opportunities to encourage and recognize results. If necessary, plan in coaching opportunities and work towards every staff member realising their full potential.

The following summarises the principles of effective delegation.

What should I delegate?

Managers or supervisors should delegate any task which somebody else can do . . .

1. ....better than they can. Managers should ensure that they are taking advantage of anybody who has work-related, specialist knowledge, so that the talents of individuals work for everyone's benefit.
2. ....cheaper than they can, because certain staff get paid less than you.
3. ....with better timing – "the less than ideal solution at the right time is better than the otherwise ideal solution at the wrong time".
4. ....as a contribution to staff training and development. If you, as a manager, feel that you cannot trust a subordinate with jobs which you know you should not be tackling, then you have a training job on your hands – and training includes delegation.

What should I not delegate?

As a manager or supervisor, you should not delegate any high-level tasks which require your full attention. Such tasks include:

1. Overall policy for your operation.
2. Overall planning.
3. Personnel matters – selection, development and appraisal of your immediate subordinates.
4. Promotion, praise and disciplinary action for your immediate subordinates.

How to delegate:

- Ensure that your staff understand the task to be achieved. Why they are doing it. What is the target? When it must be completed and to what standard?
- Give them the necessary authority – define the limits and make sure they understand them. The delegation cannot work successfully if the person has to come back repeatedly asking for permission to proceed.
- Inform any others who might be affected by your decision. A failure to do so will create unnecessary antagonism, conflict and tension.
- Your member of staff may not have carried out the delegated task before. So, you should not delegate a task without giving training or supportive coaching.
- Prepare a training plan, and remember it may take some time before they can carry out the task as well as you can.
- Allow the individual to reverse a decision themselves. Never countermand their decisions publicly.
- When the member of staff takes over the task, they accept responsibility for

their actions; you, however, must accept the accountability for any decisions you delegate.

Following up:

- Create the opportunity to take feedback on progress, but not too much as this may convey low confidence or mistrust. Review progress regularly; delegation without control is abdication.
- Give the individual as much freedom as possible to use his/her skills; don't provide answers but give some help as to where the answer may be found.
- Don't be hasty in criticising shortfalls. Maybe you wouldn't have done it that way, but it's the outcome of the delegation that is important.
- Regular appraisal of your staff must take place, with feedback as soon as possible, giving private and public praise for any task completed well.

Finally, it's important to recognise that you get what you expect – if you expect the best in people you will usually get the best; if you expect your staff to be loyal and trustworthy, they will be. The opposite of this also is true, so be clear about what you want, and believe it's possible, and the same will be true for the people who work for you.

> **11. Delegate responsibility with confidence and agree a contract of support.**

So, leadership is not the prerogative of those at the top. Enabling leadership at every level in the organisation requires trust, delegation and the skills to coach others to be more confident and independent. Empowerment with support is freeing and satisfying. Empowerment without support is uncontracted delegation and can deskill and destroy. Believing in your own strengths and the potential of others is a fundamental step to harnessing your own personal power and enabling others to realise theirs.

This power can be further enhanced by ensuring leadership at every level develops in the context of everyone, recognizing how they connect to each other. Enabling this connectedness is the next element of the Organisational Healing process.

3

Connectedness

When a part of us is injured, sick or diseased, then the whole of us is affected. Every cell in our body is connected to every other cell through nervous, circulatory and hormonal pathways. Our thoughts influence how we feel; our feelings have a direct influence on our health. Healing involves recognising the holistic nature of disease. Healing organisations involve recognising how each part, and each individual, is connected to the whole.

Team building for one department, or a new system for one function, or a recruitment drive in one area on its own, is inadequate if the objective is to create a healthy work environment which results in optimum service or productivity, one that is sustainable and fit enough to meet the challenges of a changing world.

So, will our MD recognise this, or will he attempt to change things on his own by driving the agenda single-handed?

Delectrex Limited

The canteen buzzed with anticipation. It was packed with all the managers and supervisors – around 60 altogether. This was Dave Battle's first mass public address to all his managers and the rumours were rife about what it was all about. "Cuts of some sort," whispered one. "Redundancy if we are lucky," said another – "probably another restructuring . . . ." Dave walked in followed by Babs, his PA, and Daphne, the Personnel Director.

"Morning everyone – good to see you all, and it's great to be here as your Managing Director." Dave cleared his throat and checked his papers. He had rehearsed this last night and his wife had given him the thumbs up, although he did want Ged Shaw, his consultant friend, to look at it, but he was too busy golfing!

"Delectrex Limited is a great company and is going to get even better . . . ." He went on and described the opportunities and plans for the future, being very positive and upbeat.

There was some shuffling of feet, folded arms, whispering.

"Sounds too good to be true."

"What's he after?"

"Never trust management when they are trying to butter you up."

The rumblings in the audience continued.

"Aye up, here it comes."

"Now, the only way we are going to be the best is if we all work together as one team. So, what I am asking from you is to go to your staff and ask them for their ideas for improvement – everybody's opinion is welcome and will be valued. Take your teams aside and identify what needs to change in order for things to improve. Also, I want honest feedback – I want this company to open up, so any problems or difficulties please let me or Daphne here know – together we can achieve anything!"

Dave was expecting a round of applause at this moment so paused, but all he got was a stunned silence, as one or two heads moved closer together and whispers out of the side of mouths were frustrating and distracting.

Sheila, a long serving shift supervisor whispered loudly, "He means he wants more for less – bloody typical – when does he expect us to do this, then?"

"So," ignoring the comment, Dave continued, "by next week I want hundreds of ideas from the shop floor about how to improve and become the best! With that, thanks for your time and remember – together we are one family and can beat the best because we are the best!"

Daphne starts the applause and a ripple of embarrassing clapping continued as Dave left.

"Hear that Barbara – now that's what's called motivational speaking!"

"Yes, Mr Battle."

*   *   *   *   *

Walking briskly back into his office, Dave barks "Babs – when are these decorators going to finish? Where are they now – on another tea break, I bet!"

"They are scheduled to finish this week," Babs calmly replied.

"They had better do." Dave frowned with scepticism, and turned away.

Daphne popped her head round the door with a light knock and a forced smile. "Dave – I need to see you urgently."

"Come in Daphne – any ripples from my speech yesterday? I think it went well don't you – I may do another in a few weeks to announce what ideas we are going to follow up on and . . . ."

"Dave, it's not good news – I need to shut the door."

"Do you want a coffee, Daphne?" Dave moves to his new coffee-maker machine, ignoring the concern in Daphne's voice.

"Er, no thanks – maybe something stronger later."

"What's wrong?"

"Well after your encouraging speech and suggestion that if anyone had any problems or issues then to tell me or you . . . ."

"Yes?"

"I have had three team leaders from B section in the warehouse come to see me."

"And?"

"They are making formal complaints about one of the managers, accusing him of bullying and sexual harassment!"

"Who is it?"

"Joe Danby – he's been with us for years and is very good at his job – we have never had problems from his section before."

"Well there must be something in it for three of them to approach you . . . ."

The door burst open! Dan jumps in.

"Dave – sorry for interrupting but we have an incident."

"What?!"

"The staff-side Union rep is calling a work-to-rule."

"What the hell for?" The positive feelings Dave had after his speech were now sinking fast.

"He says you are asking all staff to engage in activity that is not within their contract and not agreed – he says you are not complying with the Staff partnership agreement which states all proposals for major change should be consulted upon."

"I can't deal with this right now, you sort it – but let me know what goes on."

"They want to see you," Dan retorts.

"Daphne – sorry, can we discuss this later." The attraction of 'only Dave can sort it' was too strong.

"Sure – in the meantime I will need to start an investigation."

"Well – suspend him or something, just do something – I can be doing without this right now." He marched out and stated loudly as he left:

"Babs, I am going to sort out the Unions – back in . . . ."

"But you have a visitor waiting."

"Who – oh yes I forgot – the new supplier from Germany – apologise for me, I'll be back soon."

As Dave marched down the corridor his face getting redder and redder he bumped into his Finance Director, Dick – "Don't even ask!!! Do me a favour and go and charm our new supplier – he's in the office waiting for me."

"Supplier of what?"

"You know the auto heat switch or was it the auto cool switch – anyway one of those."

"Shouldn't Dan be doing that?"

"He's with me sorting out the bloody unions – I won't be long!!!!"

*   *   *   *   *

"You're right Ged – golf is a great game when it's going right – four good shots in a row and I have almost forgotten work. It won't last – the seventh is coming up – I've more balls in that pond than anyone else."

"Remember – it's easy to talk yourself out of a game."

"If only I could get my putter working today, your money for a change would be in my pocket, but it's strange – when one part of your game is off, it affects the whole experience."

"It doesn't have to."

"What do you mean?"

"Deal with what's wrong, head on by all means, but don't neglect the positive – celebrate the good parts and build on them; at the same time work out how to improve the rest on another day."

"That's what I am trying to do now."

"Exactly – you need to choose your moment – and in the middle of the game to start working out what's wrong and experimenting with different ways is not the best time – you need to take time out – look at it away from the heat of the game and be prepared to learn from feedback as to where you are going wrong. Each part of the game is connected to you, your thinking and feelings with all the baggage and distractions; these are also connected, influencing each part."

"Oh, boy – let's stop philosophising and play the bloody game – your honour!"

*   *   *   *   *

Back in the Club House with the customary pint . . . . "So, a challenging week then? Have the unions backed down?"

"I am meeting them again on Monday – they want to know what the process is for dealing with suggestions/ideas for improvement – and if there is a steering group, they want representation on it."

"That sounds positive."

"Bloody interference and slowing things down."

"But they want to be part of it – that needs encouraging, and what about your bully?"

"Still on suspension – he's been at it for years – why no one has spoken out before, God knows."

"Again a positive, Dave – at least you're teasing out the bad parts. Is it going on elsewhere?"

> "Hope not – I am going have to spell out what's acceptable and what isn't. I will not tolerate bullying – and they had better understand that or else!"
>
> "Have you heard yourself?"
>
> "Oh get off it, Ged – I know, it's just so frustrating – how to get everyone involved?"
>
> "Mmmm – well you don't go about it as a one-man show – here, let's have another drink and I will tell you about my favourite client, the world-famous Children's Hospital."
>
> "Just a half – I am driving . . . ."

Unfortunately, our friend, Dave Battle, in his attempt to communicate and win over his staff, fell into a few common traps:

- He assumed people shared his enthusiasm for the business.
- He believed people would enjoy coming up with new ideas.
- He underestimated the amount of resistance and cynicism in place.
- He thought he could deliver a message on his own and it would be clear to everyone.

To deliver this type of message and expect full buy-in and cooperation would require considerable groundwork to help prepare the staff to increase the chance of receptiveness and enthusiasm.

There are a few key approaches for involving all staff – the principles of which are outlined here and elaborated on in more detail in later chapters.

The challenges discussed in this chapter relate to the systematic capability of each part of the organisation being in constant and effective communication with itself and the outside world.

Making these connections creates the opportunity for individuals to contribute towards a healthy working climate in a way that they genuinely care for the future of the organisation. Aspects of connectedness we focus on in this chapter are:

- Communicating vision.
- Holistic approaches to communication.
- Communication plans.
- Communicating 'bottom up'.
- Communicating 'across'.
- Communicating 'outside in' (strategic listening).
- Connecting using listening and responding skills.

My home town is York, North Yorkshire, England – one of the most historic and beautiful cities in the UK. One day, I was walking into town for some casual shopping and I took my usual approach through the ancient 'gates' designed to keep invading Scots out in Norman times, called Monkgate.

After a few hundred yards I can't help glancing up to one of the most magnificent and beautiful Cathedrals in the World – York Minster, completed in 1472, having taken 245 years to build.

As I approached this holy splendour, I heard repetitive chiselling on stone. Being curious, I looked around two large wooden doors and sure enough here was the Minster's stone-masons yard. Two young men were sat, chiselling away at large pieces of what looked like limestone. I approached the first and asked in a friendly manner, "That looks interesting, what are you doing?"

The young man glanced at me sternly and replied, "What does it look like – I'm chipping away at this stone!" This did not encourage me to engage with him further, but I turned to the other young man who appeared to be doing an identical job and asked the same question: "That looks interesting, what are you doing?"

The young man turned to me, then glanced with a smile and a glint in his eye and pointed upwards. "I am helping restore the most beautiful cathedral in the World!"

Within this story is the essence of what we are trying to avoid and are trying to create for people at work. There is a world of difference in attitude between someone who is 'just doing their job' and someone who feels they are contributing to something greater than their 'job'. Here lies one of the secrets of getting people involved and motivated at work.

So many individuals so often feel isolated, unrecognised and undervalued. The lazy incompetence of some managers who neglect the basics of communication will eventually be asking – "Why have I got a high sickness level and absence rate? Why is morale so low?"

Let's start our exploration of connectedness by describing a unifying and potentially exciting aspect of organisational identity – the Vision.

Communicating vision

A Vision Statement is a statement of ambition. What you hope is achievable within the next three to five years. As well as the usual projection of growth, increase in quality and expanding markets and healthier profits, you need to indicate what the "pay-offs" are for everyone. This may include job security, incentive schemes, bonuses, promotion opportunities, greater sense of pride, better working conditions, etc. However, don't give false promises – always wise to give a touch of reality and make it clear that the pay-offs remain subject to the achievement of targets and an ongoing commitment to continuous improvement. It also helps to have:

a) A recognition and reward policy/approach

- A staff member of the month/year.
- A team of the month/year.
- Annual prize-giving for outstanding achievement.
- Rewards linked to personal performance.
- Training or other company visit vouchers.

All of the above, along with many other creative options for rewarding the behaviour you want, contribute to a sense of wellbeing and value. (Refer to Chapter 6, page 157). It will encourage the strength of the individuals and hence the organisation to grow stronger and for the weaknesses to be more explicit and manageable.

Given that most people spend the majority of their life at work then it makes sense to create an environment whereby people not only take pride in what they do (i.e. a Cathedral builder rather than a stone cutter) but they also get some sense of . . .

b) Social satisfaction

Lifelong friends are often created at work and many social needs, such as sharing of personal and family trials and tribulations will inevitably spill over into the work agenda. Rather than suppress this (I do know of one organisation that threatened instant dismissal over personal calls and internet surfing during work time) it is better to encourage self responsibility, managing sensitively any personal/family issues encroaching into work performance. Another important social factor is 'fun'! People want to enjoy what they do but sometimes individuals are stuck with monotonous, repetitive and less than stimulating work routines. So, ensure they have breaks, fun and comfortable opportunities to relax.

In addition to these basic needs, organisations that create an exciting, vibrant atmosphere are usually those that have a good social network with organised teams, departments, organisational events like the annual Christmas party, the social event following the AGM, the anniversary party associated with reward and recognition. Not only does this sense of occasion seep into the culture; it becomes something to look forward to and is highlighted regularly in the Company Newsletter – showing people having fun at work.

So, communicating the vision, reward and recognition and social satisfaction are some of the basic human needs addressed at work, i.e. having a sense of direction, being valued and being a member of a supportive community. In

Delectrex Limited our fictional company – very little had been done to ensure these elements were positively promoted. In fact, because of the lack of investment in these area, the signs were there that the company had turned into a *dysfunctional* family: the Christmas party that got out of hand, accusations of bullying, a staff-versus-management environment with a high level of mistrust all round.

It's no wonder that Dave Battle's attempt to motivate was akin to pouring oil onto a burning fire! He was not quite in touch with his workforce; he did not think through what the appropriate way would be to communicate his vision and ideas. Communication is an integral part of the element 'Connectedness'.

> **12. Communicate a vision that is socially inclusive and rewarding.**

Holistic approaches to communication

The most sophisticated communication system on earth (and one that we are all aware of) is the communication system within our own bodies.

When something happens to one part of our body, in the main, the rest of the body reacts and we become aware of it. When something invades our space to the extent that any one of our five senses are stimulated, we immediately begin to interpret, analyse and react.

However, even in this most sophisticated human communication system, failures and dysfunction from time to time occur. We ignore the signals resulting in things such as becoming overweight, progression of cancer, high blood pressure and a multitude of illnesses caused as a direct result of not listening to the body's feedback mechanisms.

Organisations are very similar to our human communication systems; however, they are not as sophisticated and have a greater potential for breakdown.

In every organisation I have worked in and consulted in over the last 20 years (approximately 50 different companies) the most consistent staff complaint is 'poor communication'. The majority of this criticism is directed upwards, however – further analysis has demonstrated that the problem exists at every level and between most departments – accompanied by weak or less than positive relationships with the media and stakeholders (e.g. the public and shareholders).

Communication or effective dialogue (i.e. two-way communication) is the life blood of any organisation.

Too often a memo, an email or a policy is published and it is expected that universal understanding about its meaning and significance is immediate.

This is at best, naïve – at worst, irresponsible.

As human organisms, we survive our day-to-day challenges through the mechanism of feedback. We assimilate the many, often complex, messages on a second-by-second basis to help us inform what the best decision is to enhance our situation and life.

The decisions when to eat, drink, sleep, seek out further information, ask for help, rest, speed up, slow down, laugh, cry, be entertained, learn, love, be loved, give guidance, receive guidance, applaud, speak and listen are all based on messages received in the brain, either internally or through interaction with third parties; the quality of our decisions (and their result) is dependent upon how well we respond to the messages we hear.

This is a basic survival and a life-enhancing process enabling sustained growth.

Research also indicates powerfully to us that the more an individual is informed about their situation, whether this is a state of health or how well they are getting on at work, the more opportunity and choice the individual has of taking personal responsibility and healing or improving themselves.

Organisations that take communication seriously ensure they have a communication strategy comprising of internal and external communication plans.

Communication plans

A communication plan should be able to answer the following:

1. The purpose of communication and the impact you want to have.
2. The message and its meaning.
3. Who the message is for.
4. The best method or medium to use for delivering the message.

---

13. Recognise that communication is the lifeblood of any organisation and therefore encourage everyone to be practitioners of effective dialogue.

---

1. The purpose of communication and the impact you want to have.

There are many reasons why communication needs to happen: to inform, to break down barriers, to increase motivation, to gain commitment, to ask for ideas and involvement, to consult and respect peoples positions, to negotiate, to guide, to instruct, to prevent mistakes, to educate, to name a few.

However, the clearer you are about why you are communicating and just as importantly the impact you are wanting, the more structured and the clearer the message is likely to be.

This applies to all methods of communication and is particularly relevant to how meeting agendas are structured.

Meeting management

Meetings are the most expensive management communication method, yet the one that is given least attention to in terms of training managers to design agendas and chair meetings. (See *54 Tools and Techniques for Business Excellence*, Technique N° 51, page 222)

For example, let's listen in to one of Dave Battle's meetings with his team.

"OK, final item – we are pushed for time, but this is the most important issue for today." Dave starts to shuffle his papers and prepares to propose his plans for expanding the direct sales outlet in the warehouse.

Dan comes in enthusiastically "I have done some research on this and believe we need further investment in our catalogue production."

"Hang on," says Doreen. "Before we look at that, we need to look at the development of the field sales force – I have an aging team and have started the process of recruiting two new members."

Dick looks shocked "Wait a minute – no one has told me any of this and I have prepared current direct sales figures and projections for the next two years based on existing resources."

"This is ridiculous," Dave interjects, red in the face (again). "None of this is relevant!! I'm talking specifically about the shop outlet in the warehouse – it needs refurbishing, expanding and factoring in more aggressively in terms of what we offer to the customers."

Daphne tries to ease in "But Dave, the agenda says 'Expansion of Sales Facility' which could mean . . . ."

"I haven't got time for this. Look, let's forget it for now – read my paper and we will discuss it at the next meeting." Dave picks up his papers and stands – indicating that the meeting is over.

Dave made a number of cardinal sins in agenda design and meeting management.

Not only did he leave the most important item until last on the agenda, leaving insufficient time to deal with it; he was not communicating clearly enough as to the purpose of the item. If only he had tabled the item, 'Expansion of direct sales facility', as follows:

Item	Purpose	Process	Preparation	Outcome/Impact
Expansion of direct sales facility TIME: 30 mins.	To review the current performance of the warehouse shop facility and consider its potential	To discuss a proposal for expanding the shop facility and marketing more actively	Dick: update with current shop sales figures. Dan: review existing facility in terms of potential shop expansion. Doreen: review how visibility of this facility could be increased.	Consensus as to the development of the warehouse shop facility.

By communicating clearly the purpose, process, preparation and intended outcome or impact of the agenda item, a completely different quality of meeting would have taken place. If organisations adopted the principles of effective meeting management, not only would they improve decision-making and communication – they would save probably 25% of their time, as meetings would be shorter, more effective and it will become clear that some meetings are not needed or there may be a better and more efficient way of getting a particular message across or decision made.

Whether it is in a meeting or a corridor conversation, people suffer from unconscious incompetent communication. They engage mouth before brain. If only they could pause and ask themselves, "Why am I communicating this right now, what impact am I wanting to have and how can I ensure the message gets across?" then a more conscious and competent form of communication can occur, thus the chances of effective dialogue is increased.

> **14. Introduce an effective meeting management approach. Ensure all managers are trained in the art of designing and chairing meetings. Use a common format and standard throughout the organisation.**

2. The message and its meaning

What actually do you want to say? This may be an obvious question, but what you say will be influenced by the other elements of the communication plan, i.e. the purpose, the medium and who you are communicating to.

Things to consider include:

- *Language to be used.* Is it plain English or too technical and convoluted? Simple and clear is better.
- *Tone.* Is it sensitive, directive, strong, casual, informal? What is the intention?
- *Openness.* To what extent do you want a reaction or a response? How can it be designed in a way that increases dialogue or two way interaction?
- *Interpretation.* Is the meaning clear? Could it be open to misinterpretation?
- *Timing.* What is the context, what has been said before, is this a sequence of messages? What overall effect are you wanting?

The wise communicator will pilot the message first, getting feedback with a view of shaping it to meet the needs of the audience.

3. Who the message is for

Would you give the same message in the same way to the following people?

- Operational staff.
- Senior managers.
- The Board.
- Shareholders.
- The press.
- The local MP.
- Your family.

Perhaps there may be occasional times – e.g. 'I'm redundant', 'We are bankrupt', 'I've got a promotion', 'We are in profit' – but even these deceptively simple messages would be heard more appropriately if delivered sensitively and in the context of what is understood as important from the receiver's perspective.

Tailoring your message to your audience is a crucial aspect of 'stakeholder management'. Stakeholders are those individuals or groups who have a vested interest in your success or demise. This may also involve those who potentially could have an interest in your agenda.

It's important to identify your stakeholders and assess the degree of power or influence they have and their level of interest in the message and its related agenda. (Refer to Chapter 7, page 204.)

Understanding what your audiences and stakeholders value and need will help you shape your message accordingly.

4. The best method or medium to use for delivering the message

It never ceases to amaze me how little thought people give to the *method* of communication when they want to put out a message. There is a tendency to assume a standard course of action for all communications.

For internal communication it's one of three things:

- 'Let's send an email.'
- 'Make sure it's included in the monthly briefing.'
- 'Put it on the agenda for our next meeting.'

and for external communication, it's one of two things:

- 'Let's have a publication.'
- 'Let's do a press release.'

When I witness this in meetings, I always take the opportunity to ask what the best way of communicating is, given the nature and urgency of the message.

> **15. Pay attention to how you communicate. Tailor the _m_essage appropriately for the _m_arket using the most effective _m_edia.**

It's also worth reflecting that sometimes a leader, team or department may *want* to tell everyone else about something they're doing, but does everyone want/need to know? It is important to be clear as to the purpose and value of any particular communication. Too much irrelevant information is as bad (if not worse) than not enough, because people will be overwhelmed. Better to think carefully, as a business, which bits of information are most important *and* helpful.

This, at least, begins to shape up the message and begins to ask questions as to how and when and by which means should the message go out? There are at least 54 ways to communicate effectively. The following list is a sample only, with some pros and cons for each method.

Media	Pro	Con
Email	Quick, efficient	Open to misinterpretation, one dimensional, one way
Briefing (verbal, face to face)	Same message to a group, can gauge reaction if 2 way briefing is encouraged	Not guaranteed to catch everyone, can be intimidating and not designed for getting questions and participation
Internet	Accessible, efficient	Passive, requires motivation to access, not all have full access, needs technical competence and ability
E-Learning	Can be interactive, low cost and monitored	Unless mandatory, relies on individuals to plan in time to access, not all companies facilitate this
Chat room/ Discussion forums	Can be free-flowing, informal and informative	Needs regularly stimulating and focusing on appropriate topics or can denigrate to a negative 'gossip shop' or grapevine
Telephone	Immediate, responsive	Lack of non-verbal cues, needs recording or follow up – can jump the queue regards priorities
Meetings	Controlled, time committed, recorded and scheduled	Can be a waste of time if designed and managed inappropriately, very expensive
1 to 1's	Full attention, in depth, opportunity for getting real mutual understanding	Time consuming
Video/DVD/TV	Efficient, consistent, mass market over wide geographic spread	Needs controlling and presenting in context, can be quickly out of date
Conference Calls/meetings	Same dialogue heard by several people geographically spread	Needs good technology for clear dialogue/vision, some inhibitions created if voice only, may need coaching in conference call skills
Road show	Opportunity to meet and greet, taking the message to the masses	Expensive, time out for a group of staff, value hard to measure
Newsletter	Informative, regular and up to date	Can have too many, not focused, poorly managed creating newsletter fatigue

Induction	Important early opportunity to instil values and give basic information	Sometimes late, not always followed up or matches reality
Workshops	Can be interactive, learning and informative	Needs skilled facilitators and appropriate facilities
Information packs/books	Consistency	Importance/relevance of the material may be lost
Notice boards	Cheap, easy to use, placed in accessible areas	Not always read, needs to be refreshed and updated
Events/Conferences	Can be well positioned/marketed, large scale and entertaining	Expensive and not always action oriented or followed up

The above list is not exhaustive and the purpose of including it here is to encourage the awareness and understanding that the method used to deliver the message is often as important as the message itself.

So far, we have explored Top Down (although if designed appropriately could also be bottom up) and Inside Out (stakeholder management). Three other categories remain – Outside In, Across and Bottom Up.

> **16. Listening from all 'angles' is essential to keep abreast of what's going on inside and outside of the organisation.**

Communicating bottom up

How successful you are in encouraging your staff to communicate upwards is partly dependent on how approachable managers are, and the opportunities offered for staff to express themselves. If staff opinion is valued and acted upon, then this is likely to encourage a healthy level of participation, the reverse, of course, is true.

Listening to what's really going on with your staff or team is analogous to listening to yourself.

Ignore the following at your peril:

- Increase in headaches.
- Sleepless nights.
- Loss of appetite or over-eating.

- Drinking too much.
- Increase in tension in the family.
- Loss of temper or short fuse.
- Blood pressure high.
- Increase in number of colds, flu, chest infection.
- Loss of sense of humour.
- Confused thinking.
- Cutting across others' conversation, jumping to conclusions, offering inappropriate suggestions.
- Falling asleep at work during meetings.

It's amazing how many people put up with the above before realising that it is their lifestyle decisions they are making that are contributing to the disease process.

For the same reasons many organisations stop listening and before long, they discover high sickness and absence rates, poor morale, a drop in productivity, increase in tension between unions or staff and management, increase in accidents or infection rates, increase in inter-departmental conflict, etc.

If we view the employer/employee relationship as a partnership, then, as in the case of a marriage, if you don't deal with the 'pinches' as they occur, eventually the 'crunch' will come.

The secret is having to listen out for the pinches and find ways of preventing them further.

I am reminded of the story of a man walking along the river. He noticed, in this fast running, murky tributary, a struggling swimmer crying "Help, help!" He felt a little helpless and foolish as he saw the head disappearing beneath the swirl. Then, to his relief, a brave soul on the other side of the bank jumped in and pulled the struggling swimmer out. This was amazing to see, yet later on he was witness to the same event further downstream. And again, to his relief, the same man jumped in and saved yet another person. Feeling motivated to increase his own swimming and rescue skills, he continued further downstream. Alas! Another voice – "Help, help!" As he waited for the customary rescue, sure enough, the same man came running, paused, then, to his surprise, continued to run on upstream. He shouted to the rescuer, "Wait, aren't you going to rescue this one?" The rescuer retorted with determination, "No! I'm going upstream to stop them falling in in the first place!"

So often our efforts are displaced on sorting out the failures and problems (downstream), leaving little time or resources to focus on the cause of them in the first place (upstream).

Having mechanisms to listen to staff is a significant 'upstream' preventative technique to keep in touch with the most valuable organisational resource – its people.

Of course, no mechanism is any substitute for all managers valuing the importance of listening and having the interpersonal skills to do so. (See page 86).

A popular mechanism for listening to staff is the 'staff survey'. There are many references and books that specialise in the principles of effective survey design and management, and many organisations recruit specialist consultants to conduct a survey, respecting anonymity and confidentiality. At the same time, some suppliers can offer the facility to benchmark the results with other companies in similar markets.

Suffice to say at this point, here are a few guidance tips when designing and conducting staff surveys:

1. Be clear as to the survey purpose:
   - Listening to what?
   - Staff attitude to what?
   - Progress on organisational change?
   - The extent the organisation values are understood and practised?

2. Clarify the impact you want (e.g. involvement of staff, changed perceptions, bottom up ideas for improvement, demonstration of listening and respect).

3. Involve staff early on in the design, conduct and rationale for the survey:
   - Ideally, get them to own it, give it a name by running a competition. Promise to publish and act on the results, don't let this be a one-off, ensure it is part of an ongoing strategy of improving communication.

4. Get 'survey champions' from line management:
   - Ensure there is enthusiasm to encourage survey completion and publication of results. Results can be analysed down to departmental level, giving the incentive to focus on departmental improvement.

5. Ensure union and staff representatives are involved early on to gain their commitment and reduce any suspicions.

6. Guarantee confidentiality. Repeated reassurance to staff will be needed and recruiting an outside agency for analysis and reporting will be important.

7. Pilot the questions. Use short, simple questions, do not over complicate or make the survey too long.

8. A combination different methods of delivering the survey will ensure

maximum distribution (e.g. online surveys and paper surveys).

9. Commit to a timetable for communicating the results:
   - Design forums for result discussion and a process for improving on results.
   - Highlight the positive as well as areas for improvement.

10. Review the whole process, listen to feedback and design in improvements to the survey design and management process for the following year.

> **17. Make your staff survey an integral part of a continuously improving communication process.**

Communicating across

Are the following familiar?

- Departmentalism
- Silo mentality
- Management versus staff
- Sales versus order fulfilment/production
- Doctors versus management
- Pilots versus management
- Engineering versus finance
- Spend our budget quick or we will get it cut

If so, you have or are experiencing a disjointed and dysfunctional organisation – one where teamwork outside one's own department or function/profession has been neglected or efforts to improve have been ineffective.

This situation has probably occurred due to a number of reasons, but is usually associated with the following:

- Neglect of organisation wide communication and the importance of team work for the service of the business/customer/client.
- Lack of creativity regarding staff rotation and job variability.
- Lack of multidisciplinary project management.
- Poor leadership models.
- Inability to face difficult cross-departmental issues resulting in empire building and resource protection.

Breaking down barriers between departments and professionals is important if sustainable healing and hence optimum business performance is to be achieved.

This can be achieved by creating a climate of internal customer-supplier relationships, i.e. everyone recognising that they are a customer and supplier of each other.

There is a direct correlation between how staff treat and relate to each other and the ultimate customer/client experience.

This climate can be created if supported by clear communication and positive role modelling from the top. The clear communication needs to reinforce the importance of teamwork, the core business focus being customer satisfaction, the value of teamwork and the essential ingredients of trust and respect for each other. This will significantly contribute to excellent customer service both internal and external.

Words, however, need to be supported by experience, opportunity to work differently and good coaching. This often involves negotiation, compromise, conflict management and sharing performance management results and experience.

Two exercises I use in this context are ice breakers followed by an internal negotiation exercise.

The ice breaker involves up to 12 individuals, all from different departments, placing their names and function on a 'map'. Central to this 'map' is the end customer. The individuals need to place themselves close to or far away from the customer – depending on how much they deal with them. They then need to draw a red line to anyone else whom they deliver a service to – this includes information, completed forms, materials, etc. They then need to draw a green line to anyone they expect to get a service from. This, in itself, can be quite illuminating – however, the most challenging part of the exercise is to come. They then need to indicate their own personal level of customer satisfaction related to the internal service they are given.

This ice breaker usually gets the attention! Following this, after some appropriate input ensuring the context of the exercise is understood, a step-by-step internal customer/supplier negotiation takes place. This results in a contract of improvement between relevant players. Further details of the exercise can be found in *54 Tools and Techniques for Business Excellence,* Technique N° 27, page 124 and Technique N° 12, page 53).

Communicating outside in – strategic listening

The Cathedral builder felt connected to the ultimate goal and understood what his contribution was. The stonecutter was miserably isolated in completing his task (refer to page 70). Creating this internally connected environment is so important to enable each part to communicate and work with each other, thus creating a team of cathedral builders, rather than stonecutters.

However, this is not enough as every organisation also needs to understand and appreciate its connectedness with the outside world, i.e. its community, the market and changing forces.

---

18. Strategically review the business of the organisation at least twice a year – know what the influences are now and are likely to be in the future.

Without this connection and intimate knowledge – the business of any organisation could suffer from institutionalised navel-gazing and wake up one day and wonder why their customers are leaving them in droves and the books begin to look unhealthy.

Every organisation needs to review its strategic position at least once, if not twice, a year. This review can be a combination of internal and external listening.

This can be done by facilitating a **SWOT** and **PESTLE** analysis, i.e. asking a team to identify the following:

Strengths   What are we good at, what's our reputation, can we make more of this?

Weaknesses   Where are we vulnerable, what do we need to develop, where are we at risk?

Opportunities   How can we develop new business, create new markets, grow and improve our performance?

Threats   What is our competition doing, what changes are on the horizons which ones have implications for us?

If the above **SWOT** analysis is done in the context of a **PESTLE** analysis, the appropriate external listening can add value to major decisions concerning business development, i.e.

Political   Will a change in government effect our business? If so, what is the likely direction of travel and can we prepare for this?

How do we ensure we have our local MP supporting us?

How can we ensure we have a positive profile with our local council?

Are we managing the media positively and proactively?

Do we consult appropriately with our community?

Economical   How is the general economy affecting business demand and development?

Do we have sufficient contingency to cope with a down turn?

What are the economical projections and are we positioned appropriately to take advantage of this?

What are the possible cost changes in materials, fuel, energy supply etc – have we factored this into our business plans?

Social   To what extent do changes in social trends affect our business, i.e. fashion, customer expectations, customer attitude and behaviour?

How are demographic variations relevant, i.e. growth of new towns, housing, aging population, etc.?

What local changes are likely to impact our business and could this affect where we are likely to recruit most of our employees from?

Technical   Are we making the most of technology?

Can we utilise better the technology we have?

Is it fit for the next three to five years?

What investment do we need to ensure we are up to date and technically savvy?

How can our customers and suppliers take advantage of our technology to enhance service?

Are we appropriately visible on the internet?

Is our intranet enhancing internal customer/supplier relationships?

Legal   Are our governance arrangements robust, auditable and ethical?

Are we geared up to ensure we are up-to-date with a continual changing legal environment?

Do we comply with all relevant legislation?

Environment   Do we have a 'sustainability' policy – one where all matters concerning damage limitation to the environment and where possible contributions to enhancing the environment is made?

Do we all actively consider reducing our carbon footprint?

Are we continually seeking efficient ways of improving our business in partnership with the vision for a greener and healthier environmental climate.

The resulting conclusions from the answers to the above **PESTLE** questions need feeding into a strategic business plan. The connecting process does not stop here. Translation of these insights into a form of communication for all staff will help each employee continue connecting their individual contribution to the bigger picture, thus increasing the chance of staff embracing rather than resisting change.

> **19. Connect strategy to business plan to priorities to key performance indicators to personal objectives. Ensure the stonecutters know they are building a cathedral. (See page 70.)**

Connecting using listening and responding skills

The interpersonal skills of leadership that facilitate meaningful connection with people in the organisation are often referred to as soft skills – yet they are the hardest management competency to practise well. Effective and meaningful dialogue is dependent upon the ability to listen and respond in a way that creates business enhancing relationships. Increasingly these skills are being recognised as core competencies in today's Leadership Development agenda. A summary of these skills are given here:

Non-verbal communication (NVC)

A large percentage of any verbal message is conveyed non-verbally. Sensitivity to how NVC can enhance or diminish the message will increase the chance of

86

achieving rapport. Some examples are:

Square   Face the person you are in dialogue with.

Spatial sensitivity   Not too close or too distant – be aware of cultural variations.

Pace   The speed of conversation needs to be appropriate to keep attention, understanding and match the pace of the responder. Sometimes, you may need to break the rapport by changing the pace to help others either speed up or slow down.

Eye   Eye contact needs to be appropriate. Avoid staring and looking away. Be as natural as possible.

Lean   Leaning forward will show interest and encourage others to tell their story.

Tone   The nature of your voice can convey harshness and coldness. Try warm and inviting.

Mirror   Match the others' posture, mirror-like. This conveys being in tune, having rapport.

Open   Having an open posture will encourage others to open up. Avoid folded arms, legs and crouched or tense postures.

Relax   Be aware and sensitive to your own and others non verbal cues but above all, relax, be genuine, be yourself.

Paraphrasing

Useful to repeat back your understanding of what you have heard in short phrases – avoid interpreting, judging or analysing.

Reflecting

Listen out for and repeat back key words and feelings you think may be significant. Get them to confirm or otherwise the significance of these.

Empathy

The most important interpersonal skill is to demonstrate support and understanding. It involves understanding the other person from their perspective.

Seeing the world from their point of view. Standing in their shoes without the complication of your feelings or experiences. It is important to distinguish between empathy and sympathy.

Sympathy is about feeling sorry for someone else based on your assumption of having a similar experience and how you felt. In effective dialogue terms – this is not helpful.

Empathy is experienced by stating how you think someone feels and why, i.e. "You feel . . . . because . . . ."

Rarely expressed skilfully in day-to-day business, its barriers include a 'macho' reluctance to be open about feelings. Feelings are major indicators of what's really going on; they are clues to drivers, motivators, barriers and real problems. There is a correlation between one's ability to express one's own feelings and the ability to recognise and acknowledge feelings in others.

Open questions

Asking open questions as opposed to closed questions is easier said than done. An open question is one where there has to be more than a 'yes' or 'no' answer. It involves asking a question without pre-judging what the answer might be.

Try to avoid asking questions that are leading (based on the opinion of what the answer should be from the questioner's perspective) or based on curiosity (seeking information to satisfy the questioner).

Open questions in the context of developing a healing organisation relate to enabling others to tell their story in their own terms, identify problems and have opportunities for self-advancement.

Summarising

The ability to listen to an individual or team story, then summarise it, pulling all the key points together, is a powerful way of drawing things to a conclusion or moving on to a different phase of the dialogue.

Challenging skills

Essential to enable others to see their own blind spots and break through their own resistance. (Refer to Chapter 7 and also to *54 Tools and Techniques for Business Excellence'* Technique N° 44, page 187).

These skills are a prerequisite if you want to achieve effective dialogue in the following:

- 1:1 personal development reviews.

88

- Chairing and participating in meetings.
- Identifying customer needs.
- Negotiating.
- Contracting.
- Life.

> **20. Ask your managers to 'connect' by demonstrating high levels of listening and responding abilities. Make the level of interpersonal skill ability discussable.**

In summary; as we understand the impact of how every cell in our body is connected to each other, our feelings therefore have a direct impact on our health. Organisations that achieve 'healing' status understand this. They invest specific time and resources in improving their communication systems inside and out. Their leaders are model communicators, listening and responding appropriately, and are not afraid of boldly encouraging the expression of feelings in order to achieve meaningful and long-lasting relationships.

These feelings are likely to be clues as to the motivators or drivers of behaviour and must be taken into consideration if the purpose of communication is to get everyone involved and motivated toward achieving the organisational vision. This level of 'ownership' is a significant challenge and will be explored in the next chapter.

4

Ownership

The most powerful human motivator is the desire to survive. To live on. When our lives are threatened we do our utmost to protect. Often, too late, we recognise we have neglected our health, smoked too much, drunk too much, not taken enough exercise, eaten too much food, etc. However, if the doctor turned and said to you, "You will die in a few months if you don't stop . . . ." (or "if you don't start . . . ."), then you are more than likely to comply.

For some, this message has been given for years, yet our brains are amazing defenders of the status quo – denying the stark facts to protect the current situation.

Organisations and people in organisations are the same.

It is easy for the manager or team member or worker to deflect anything wrong with their work situation and blame it on the boss, or another department or other facts that are perceived as beyond their control. The situation is often worse in that somehow individuals think that things will get better; someone else is responsible for improving the work situation. It is almost as if the individual discovers they have liver or kidney failure, or a gangrenous toe, but decides that, somehow, it will get better on its own, or someone will come to the rescue.

Someone usually does when it comes to our health, but unless we take responsibility for keeping healthy, then reoccurrence of the same problem is likely.

Within organisations, individuals need to recognise that they are part of the whole, that they affect everything else and that they are responsible for a healthy working environment.

Enabling individuals to believe they are a valuable and valued part of the organisation and are empowered to influence it for the better, is a challenging element of the quest for a healing organisation.

No doubt Dave Battle has, by now, made progress, but has he got that strength of ownership, commitment and passion from sufficient numbers of his team and managers to coach and facilitate the rest of the organisation – thus raising the game, increasing productivity and efficiency?

Delectrex Limited

Dave Battle, the ambitious new managing director of Delectrex Limited had survived his first six months. He had managed to reassure his fellow executives, avoided another strike, saved a major contract, dealt with a serious case of bullying and introduced a regular briefing session for all staff. His Secretary, Barbara, had not been in tears for almost two weeks now and he had started going to the 'Grapevine' for a drink with his team on Friday evenings straight after work. So as he sat in his newly decorated office feeling quite smug about his achievements, his attention was distracted to the car park where two of his team seem to be in a very animated, robust conversation just outside the office. Dave quietly opened his window to listen in.

"If you spent less time at conferences and more time finding out what your sales team were doing, we wouldn't be in this mess."

"How dare you, Dan! That's not fair – you, at the end of the day, are responsible for stock control. How are we to know that one particular product line was not available if you don't ensure the information is up-to-date on the system?" Doreen was a formidable opponent in any disagreement.

"You know there is a one-week time lag on updates – ever since Dave had the bright idea of changing the system!" Dan defended strongly.

"Oh, so it's his fault, is it?" '*Anyone's but mine*' she thought, with increasing tension.

"Well, it's not mine!" Dan became aware of being watched and lowered his voice and walked away from the building.

"Do you think he heard us?" Doreen glanced to the side.

"You know, Doreen, I am beginning to care less and less. This place used to be a good working environment. It's just gone from bad to worse."

Doreen, now in a more receptive mood, asked, "Are you sure it's still not just sour grapes for not getting the job? Would you have done anything differently?"

Dan, now wanting to end the conversation and get back to work, replied "I certainly would, yes, indeed . . . ."

*   *   *   *   *

Dave was surprised and disappointed to have overheard two of his team arguing. He had thought everyone was getting on so well, and the session last Friday in the pub had been light-hearted and fun. Was he missing something? Perhaps it was time for a heart-to-heart with each of his team – cards on the table. Dave mused over the best way of approaching them and considered what he wanted from these conversations.

At that moment, Barbara popped her head around the door.

"Er, Mr Battle, there is a Police Officer here to see you."

"What does he want?"

"*She* says it's personal."

"Oh, right – you'd better show her in!"

*   *   *   *   *

For nearly a year now, the 'gang of four', as they were known to their team mates, had been running a successful little business selling off wire, components, tools and (most ingeniously) small robot-like structures made from components which seem to have become a bit of a collector's item amongst employees' children and their friends.

The ringleader, Rob, a shift supervisor now for 20 years, had cunningly managed to gain the cooperation of several staff to secrete on a regular basis enough stock and materials to run a regular 'car boot' at the local market.

Unfortunately, a complaint from a child's mother in a distressed state claimed that the toy robot figures were dangerous, having just taken a nut and bolt out of her four-year-olds' mouth! This resulted in the parts being traced to come from the Delectrex Limited factory.

The resulting investigation led to the suspension of the gang of four, and a crisis meeting of the top team was called.

Dave's tone was serious, deliberate and to the point.

"I don't really know what's going on, do I? I don't know you, I don't know my staff and I don't believe the majority of staff care for the future of this company."

Dan stirred, ready for a fight.

Daphne got ready to calm things down.

Dick nodded in agreement and Doreen rolled her eyes.

"It's time we put cards on the table. If we are going to pull this business round, somehow we all have to take more responsibility in its future – and I mean everyone – every single member of the organisation . . . ."

*   *   *   *   *

"You know, I think I'm going to give this game up, Ged." Dave, now on his second pint of beer was in a more than usually depressed mood.

"Come on Dave, I've known you play worse!"

"Not much Ged – I think it may be time for a new set of clubs. Most people get their clubs fitted these days – that may be my problem."

"It might help." Ged replied in a conciliatory tone.

"Or maybe it's the balls – I never pay attention to the choice of ball but I read the other day it can make a difference."

"I don't think so Dave – I think the weather has a lot to do with today."

"You managed it OK," Dave grumbled.

"Mmmmm, that's right!" Ged smiled smugly.

"OK – if it's not the clubs, balls or weather – it's got to be work! If it wasn't for this job, I would certainly be in a better mood!"

"Or perhaps it's just us?" Ged looked into his pint.

"What do you mean?"

"At the end of the day, we choose how much we practise, how we handle the distractions of the day, what our mood is and how well we adapt to the conditions. A good player rarely blames external factors on other people."

"You know, Ged, I'm ahead of you for a change – this is exactly where I am at work at the moment. By the way, have you come across any cute little metal robots made out of nuts, bolts and wires?"

At last, Dave Battle recognised he can't force change through. His team and his staff need to be trained in the skills and competencies related to becoming a high quality and healthy business.

In his blind enthusiasm, Dave had driven through changes in the organisation with some success, but had neglected to pause and listen to what was really going on.

It seemed he was still not in touch with shopfloor reality and had not really considered how his team felt about changes and the impact on each other.

In this chapter, the importance of the following is described:

- Practise what you preach
- Board development
- Executive team development
- Facilitator training
- The ongoing development of facilitators and action learning
- The cost of quality and failure

Practise what you preach

My clients tend to be long-term – when they move into a new job or company, shortly after starting they will often ask me to help them take stock.

This usually involves pausing, doing a strategic review, finding out what's really going on and building a greater commitment to work together.

This is a healthy intervention. However, I have known several MDs and senior executives who continue to blame their team, the staff, the economic/market situation – even their customers – before taking an honest look at themselves and how they are making decisions and impacting the business in the way they are working with others. This level of denial, which is often driven by an urge to control and demonstrate authority and power, will eventually lead to dysfunction and disease.

It's often a crisis or incident that creates a wake-up call – for example, the resignation of a critical staff member, an increase in sickness due to stress, an instance of professional misconduct resulting in legal or criminal proceedings, a sudden increase in customer complaints, team members walking out of meetings, strike action, and so on.

All these are symptoms of an organisation that has put more emphasis on delivering quantity and not enough on quality and prevention or customer/staff care.

The drive for success is commendable, but if it is felt by only a few people, driving blindly, then the ownership of the need for success and the commitment to excel is displaced, i.e. dependent on those driving and not shared. This is also likely to exclude the many people with talent and resources who would be more than willing to contribute and show what they can do.

This results in a dependent culture which will always be exposed to resistance to change, cynicism and the development of a blame culture when things go wrong.

The challenge for these organisations is to get the ownership and commitment for organisational success in the hearts and minds of everyone in the organisation in a climate of no blame and continuous learning and improvement. It requires positive modelling from the top and a systematic approach to developing the organisation in all its activities.

In order to get everyone engaged, some form of active communication needs to touch every heart and mind in the organisation. This needs to be done in a way that delivers a consistent message, at the same time demonstrating in the way the message is delivered that the 'authors' of the message practise what they preach. This must be reflected in their behaviours as well as their words. For example:

Message	Behaviours
We want an open and honest, no blame culture.	Managers go out of their way to praise and are skilled in facilitating positive reviews of failure, turning it around to an improvement agenda.
We value your ideas and need your contributions.	Managers are skilled at listening and coaching staff – to help them develop their ideas. They support and follow through improvement initiatives and give appropriate recognition.
We are one team.	Co-operation and support for one another is visible. Information is openly shared.
Respect for each other and our customers.	Demonstrated through an internal customer supplier relationship and the customer being central to any service decision.
Effective communication is essential to quality.	Managers are expert communicators and there is a focused effort to continuously improve communication at every level. Managers are visible, accessible and approachable. Staff have opportunities to give honest feedback and this feedback is responded to.

---

21. Check that your behaviours as a team are consistent with the messages you send out.

It can be seen from this illustration of message/behaviour relationship that before any decision to cascade to everyone 'a plea for their commitment and involvement' (witness the early mistake made by our MD Dave Battle in Chapter 3), investment needs to be directed to a critical mass of managers and 'facilitators' to ensure there is some tangible evidence that things are already changing and the organisation has the capacity to deliver the message and follow through on the intended improvement initiatives. Direct engagement with key groups of staff such as unions and professional staff is also important at this stage.

The three significant development programmes I involve my clients in are:

- Board Development.
- Executive Team Development.
- Facilitator Training.

Board development

To embark upon an organisation-wide programme of involvement for all staff will need endorsement from the Board for a number of reasons;

1. It may need financial support/investment.
2. It will be important that the non-executives and executives are seen to behave in a way that supports the 'aspired' culture.
3. The chair and non-executives may be called upon to speak about the process, either in giving recognition to individuals or teams, or speaking to the media.

Embarking upon an organisation-wide culture change process is not a soft option. In fact, there may be 'safer' options that deliver just enough. However, commitment to this process will depend on how ambitious the Board are. To what extent do they want to 'be the best', be a 'top quality organisation' and be recognised as 'world class'?

If the answer to these is positive, then to realise this ambition will require a significant level of organisation-wide investment.

Some tough decisions on the way may also be needed. The more explicit an organisation is about its values and expected behaviours, the more likely it is that discrepant behaviours will become visible. This will create expectancy and a demand that the process of personal performance management and discipline is conducted effectively and fairly.

Also, by investing in the development of managers and especially in 'facilitators', you immediately increase expectation as to what is possible regarding increased job satisfaction and/or career development options. Appropriate application of new skills and behaviours will occur if the organisation changes positively at a pace whereby developed individuals are able to put their new-found skills into practice with good effect. However, if the programme falters or the organisation does not change at a pace which allows the facilitators of the change (whoever they may be) to achieve visible results, then it is predicted that a proportion of the more capable individuals will successfully gain promotion elsewhere (facilitator skills are very marketable). So, commitment to invest is not without its risks, and the more explicit the risks are, the greater the commitment to the decision for a full-blown organisation-wide change programme. All these issues need to be explored in the context of strategic ambition of the organisation and the operational capability of putting strategy into action.

Emotional commitment and buy-in to creating a sustainable high-quality business needs to happen. Each Board member needs to genuinely care about the organisation's future to the extent that they are prepared to put their heart and soul into leading the agenda for change and improvement.

This level of emotional commitment is not created at a regular Board meeting. A 'Time Out' usually with an overnight stay away from the work environment, or at least quality time together over an informal dinner, will help in creating a challenging workshop environment in which the ideas and proposals as to the way forward can be robustly and creatively challenged. A test of commitment can be useful by revisiting the decision a week later, away from the workshop environment, which can be intensive and sometimes emotive.

**22. Create the opportunity for Non-Executive
Directors to be ambassadors with insight to the
process of organisational healing.**

Executive team development

The 'team at the top' must be seen to be excellent. They need to be living examples of good practice, leadership role models, approachable, reassuring, trusted, respected and visible to all staff.

A team may consist of a collection of competent individuals, but still not merit the description 'excellent'. Each executive will have their own specialist area of expertise; HR, Finance, Operations, Sales and Marketing, Manufacturing, Engineering, Nursing/Clinical, etc. However, they also need to be role models for leadership and team work.

The Chief Executive is crucial in shaping the individuals to become a high-performing team. He or she needs to believe passionately that the vision of the 'healing organisation' is the ideal, the dream, the motivating and unifying goal that can help drive the business forward.

They also need to be clear as to the reason, the rationale, the driving force or the strength of purpose.

One or more of the following drivers have been the main reason why my previous clients have embarked upon a systematic healing approach to organisation development:

- Two organisations into one – the need for one culture.
- Reputation damaged – need to recover our pride.
- Worst performing organisation in the area/country – need to turnaround to survive.
- Modernisation – to transform the way we do business.
- Take-over/merger – to develop trust at every level.
- New organisation, change of boundary and purpose – establish ourselves and become fit for purpose.
- Major customers expectation for quality – to meet customers' demands and comply with quality standards.
- To become the best, lead and shape – to contribute to the National agenda, to be a pioneer and exemplar of world class practice.
- Institutionalised blame culture and dysfunctional practice.

Whatever the driver, the reason for change needs to be couched in positive, motivating terms and owned strongly by each executive team member. This then becomes the foundation contract that each individual buys into and continuously refers to in their quest for excellence. This standard of excellence captured in the spirit of being a 'healing organisation' needs to be expressed in reality between themselves.

Essentially, this means practising and becoming what they want for the whole organisation, on a day-to-day basis as a team, in the way they communicate, behave to one another, make decisions and are visible to the rest of the organisation.

Developing a top team occurs through dedicated bespoke design and input, addressing each individual's personal development needs as a leader in a team environment. Many approaches are available. I have used a combination of the following in the past:

- One-to-one needs analysis based on core leadership competencies.
- Myers Briggs Type Indicator$^{®}$ (MBTI$^{®}$) analysis.
- Belbin® Team Roles analysis.
- Lean quality assessment questionnaires – MWA (UK) Ltd$^{©}$.
- Team problem-solving – outdoor pursuits.
- Facilitator training for top teams.
- Coaching skills.
- Team based strategic review process including vision building.
- Creative/alternative approaches using dramatic acting out using established plays/scripts.
- Biography/timeline analysis.

> **23. Be clear as to the reason for embarking upon organisation wide development. Ensure real choice and commitment by exploring alternative options.**

There are many approaches available to team building. Suffice to say that spending dedicated time investing in the top teams to become examples of excellence is well worth the time, effort and cost. Especially if that investment is then dedicated to modelling and coaching the rest of the organisation.

The team events that make a difference are those often talked about or referred back to for years – they become a watershed in how a team works together brought about by a combination of new insight into what they need to do differently to move the organisation forward and getting to know each other much better, therefore increasing the range of options for creative debate and decision-making.

Some examples of creative team events I have facilitated include:

Acting yourself

Using a scene from Noel Coward's *Hay Fever* and working with a professional producer, we spent two days coaching a team to act out the scene by each taking a particular role.

Hay Fever is a comic play written by Noel Coward in 1924. Best described as a cross between high farce and a comedy of manners, the play is set in a British country house in the 1920s, and deals with the four eccentric members of the Bliss family and their outlandish behaviour when they each invite a guest to spend the weekend. The self-centred behaviour of the hosts finally drives their guests to flee while the hosts are so engaged in a family row that they do not notice their guests' furtive departure.

The roles were given to individuals that best fit in relation to their personal character and position in the team. A combination of fun, laughter, creativity, pushing the boundaries, doing something different, intensive teamwork with a shared goal and a great sense of satisfaction and increased confidence following a successful performance resulted in a great occasion!

The debrief that followed created new insights into each others' strengths and how they were being used to varying degrees in the organisation. It broke down barriers and resulted in a level of honesty never achieved before.

Outdoor pursuits

On another occasion a team of hard-nosed sales people, engineering and senior managers were brought down to earth when they were forced to work in a team to navigate a course that involved orienteering through woods, mountain-biking, boating and problem-solving over various obstacles. Again, the critical element of this two-day event was the debriefing and application of learning to issues at work.

Treasure trailing

A simple walk around a strange town to find answers to questions *en route* can create a range of issues when an established team is split in two and sent in opposite directions, competing to see who finishes first with most accurate answers. Issues of competitiveness, decision-making, delegation, best use of resources and leadership styles can be highlighted through a creative and robust debrief. I have used this on many occasions as an icebreaker or to create an interval in a two or three-day 'time out' event.

The examples given are a few of the more creative options among the many traditional approaches that most organisations go for.

---

24. Invest in your team being a 'model team' – design bespoke events based on real team needs in the context of what you are trying to achieve as a business.

I believe for an organisation to achieve 'healing' status, it must tap into its creative side, think differently and take risks in doing new things – this in itself will create renewed optimism and motivation for achieving extraordinary things – more of this later.

Some of the most effective culture change processes I have been involved with have been enhanced and sustained because the top team agreed to be trained alongside other members of staff, thus showing their vulnerability, willingness to learn and determination to ensure that hierarchy and status should not be a barrier to working or learning together.

Facilitator training

To facilitate is, essentially, to 'ease' the process of doing business. For an organisation to achieve sustainable excellence, then they will need their own 'healers' or facilitators – individuals trained in the art of working smarter and in the application of the full range of business and quality enhancing tools and techniques.

This is the most cost effective way of increasing the level of competence and improving the performance of all aspects of organisational life. It reduces any dependency on external suppliers and becomes the source of a critical momentum of positive change.

When the 'facilitators' work together they share their learning and experiences which can then feedback to a 'strategic forum' (sometimes called a steering group). The facilitators inform them on progress and identification of key areas for improvement.

Selection of facilitators

The criteria for selection include peer respect, ability to work well in groups, visibility because of their efforts to promote change, interpersonal skills and willingness to lead and shape the organisational agenda.

Note that there is no mention of status or position. The ideal mix of a group of facilitators should be taken from all levels.

Some of the most creative and productive groups I have trained involve medical consultants working with hospital porters, chief executives working with nursing assistants, secretaries working with senior professional staff.

Facilitator training involves creating a learning network whereby the organisational healing process is demonstrated through mutual respect and value of each others' strengths. Thus, each individual through a process of training and development begins to realise their full potential. It is this direct experience of development that I ask them to pass on to others to create the opportunity for everyone in the organisation to develop and learn. When a 'facilitator' resource is unleashed into the organisation, the potential is phenomenal!

The nature and process of training and developing facilitators

The length, intensity and nature of facilitator training will vary depending on who trains them, the culture of the organisation, the challenges it faces, and the individuals involved. It can be from three days to three months training.

Over the years, I have tailored a formula for facilitator training that meets the needs of the organisation (it is realistic in terms of time taken and cost) and also its context (it is designed into an ongoing development network using Action Learning as a basis for support).

Action Learning involves a small group facilitated in a specific manner designed to encourage insight into individuals' effectiveness at work at the same time promote ongoing learning about how groups work. We will discuss how this key element of organisational healing works in more detail later.

Facilitator training is not something to be taken lightly. The nature of facilitator training should challenge the most seasoned professional as it is not just about learning new techniques. It requires the individual to experience in depth what the concept of a 'healing organisation' means to themselves.

So before they are placed in a position to facilitate others, they must first of all facilitate themselves and each other – they must understand how they impact on others, raise their awareness of own style of management and leadership and decision-making preferences.

They need to understand their current level of listening, coaching and problem-solving skills, then design a personal development plan to continue working on throughout their time as a facilitator, if not their personal career as a whole.

The impact of facilitator training on an individual should increase confidence, assertiveness, ability to influence groups and help others improve through coaching and training.

The following components of facilitator training can be designed in three 2½-day workshops, followed by ongoing commitment for meeting half a day a month in Action Learning Sets.

- Listening, questioning and challenging skills.
- The power of non-verbal communication.
- Utilising a personal development framework for personal direction and career development.
- Feedback skills.
- Coaching skills.
- Appreciation of the full range of leadership styles and increase options for choosing appropriate style to suit the situation.
- Transformational leadership.
- Problem-solving.
- Project management within a problem-solving/prevention framework.
- Insight to own preferences and style of influencing groups.

- Understanding group dynamics and how to impact or shape group behaviour.
- Team development.
- Stress management.
- Time management.
- Delegation skills.
- Presentation and training skills.
- Workshop design skills.
- Ability to present, train and coach project teams in some of the tools and techniques described in *54 Tools and Techniques for Business Excellence.*

For a facilitator to be successful, they need to work in an environment of legitimacy – i.e. everyone understands the role they play, the value they offer and why it's important to have this resource.

Facilitators are, at first, vulnerable, as the organisation will initially want to rely on the facilitators inappropriately. The facilitators need to be robust enough to challenge these demands and avoid colluding with any dependency.

I include here a description of the role of a facilitator in the context of working with projects and project leaders.

> **25. Train your own facilitators in the process of organisational healing and the tools and techniques for business excellence.**

Beginning work: agreeing a 'contract' to facilitate

Contact for work as a facilitator may be initiated by a Manager's invitation, by a group of staff in a department or unit, or on the advice of a third party. In each of these cases, the facilitator often enters the situation with a slightly different agenda for the task ahead.

The facilitator's activities and behaviour in the early stages of a relationship with a client (e.g. a project leader) are crucial in setting future direction and tone. They need careful planning in the light of the facilitator's interpretation of the 'agenda'. Facilitators need to establish to their own satisfaction the answers to **four** related questions, described in Figure 7.

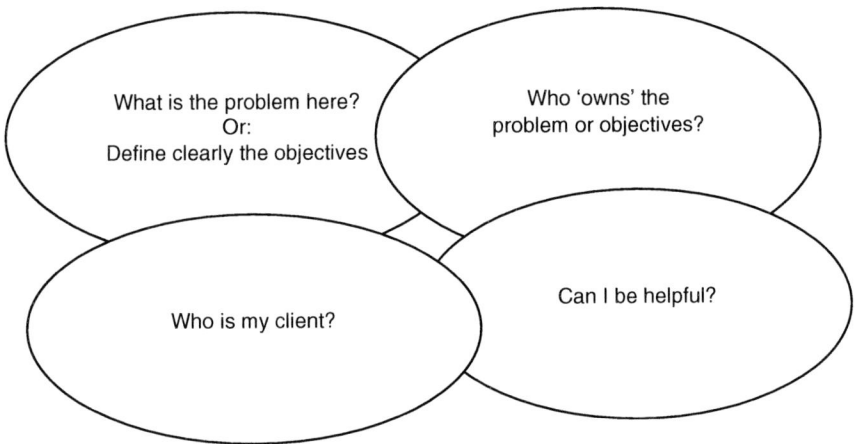

Figure 7. Four questions a facilitator must ask

In clarifying these basic questions, some major issues must be confronted and managed within the developing relationship. Listening carefully to the client is crucial at this stage, especially in terms of:

Content: What are the facts you are hearing? What information are you learning? What are the client's expectations? What is the intended outcome?

Process: What issues come across about control, authority and trust? What methods and/or approach is intended or proposed?

Feelings: What clues to these are you picking up? What's the level of motivation, commitment, risk and anxiety.

The facilitator will need to address both the interpersonal issues and the tangibles on contracting with the client at this early stage.

Interpersonal issues

These are likely to include:

Anxiety and tension levels

This is especially the case if the facilitator is inexperienced, when both facilitator and client may worry about risks of failure. This is best handled by careful structuring of any intended meeting or workshop, by setting a clear agenda, by clarifying objectives and how time will be managed.

Trust

Facilitators can best handle this by being open about their motivation and by trying to elicit the same openness from the client. It is helpful to clarify how you will be able to exert influence and control over the session – and build this in to the workshop or meeting design. The facilitator could well talk about the client's role as leader and whether, for example, he or she wants to be in groups, or to observe; discussion could cover the points at which the facilitator will ask the client to summarise progress, to give him or her feedback or to make a short input contribution.

Developing a partnership relationship between client/project leader and facilitator is often very positive and mutually developmental.

Confidence in personal expertise

The facilitator should handle this by showing a professional approach at every stage – in the planning, discussion, documentation, and so on. Doing the homework is very important.

Contracting tangibles

This covers what the client expects of the facilitator, and it is best to be explicit in discussing such matters as:

Outcomes

What outcomes are desired and how will the facilitator and the client recognise these when they are achieved?

Resource

How much time, money, support, and so on is available? Are there limitations upon its use.

Roles

Are the respective roles clearly defined?

The contracting process – '7 Es'

(Guidance for project leaders)

Entry   Where do I find a facilitator?

Explanation   Let me tell you a little about the project.

Establishing Interest   Is it something you would be interested in helping with?

Expectation   What's the role of the facilitator in this?

Explicit Roles   How should we work together?

Engagement   When should we start and what should we do first? What is the time/resource commitment?

Evaluation   How is it going?

Facilitator support – Stage 1 supportive options

1. Help the project leader think through the Stage 1 template items a) to m). (See page 145).
2. Skills required – listening, open questions, clarification, summarising, challenging. May need some visioning prompts (see page 52) when asking 'intended outcomes, purpose'.
3. Good idea to have examples of previously filled in Stage 1 forms. (Page 145.)
4. Help the project leader think through criteria for team selection. Avoid your own suggestions.
5. Agree your role regards support in the first project team meeting. Help the project leader design the first meeting.

Some useful questions for facilitators to ask during project meetings

The following questions enable the team to move through the project in a structured way.

1. Present

1.1 Why is the present situation so unacceptable?
1.2 So, what is actually causing the problems?
1.3 Who has the most knowledge of the background/the facts/the history?
1.4 Could someone summarise the essence of what's really going on?

1.5   What are the main pieces of the jigsaw here – can we start putting it together?

1.6   Out of this complex picture – what are the two or three critical issues to address?

1.7   Are you sure you are not missing anything?

1.8   If you stood back and took a really critical eye on what you have – is it the complete picture?

2.   Future

2.1   So, what you plan to change is . . . . ?

2.2   Ideally, how would you like the situation to be?

2.3   You will know that this is successful when you see what happening?

2.4   Where does the commitment lie for this?

2.5   What would be the best possible outcome?

2.6   Tell me again, what will success look like on the ground?

2.7   What is your own personal benchmark for success in all this?

3.   Action

3.1   So, what is your plan for change?

3.2   What would your criteria be for evaluating this change?

3.3   The main forces pushing for this are . . . what?

3.4   The main factors preventing this are . . . what?

3.5   The people you need to involve most are . . . who?

3.6   How will you gather support?

3.7   What is your timetable for the change?

3.8   What are the resources you will need?

3.9   This has implications for other areas, what are they?

3.10 What would be the worst thing that could possible go wrong?

3.11 What actually is your first step – when exactly will this happen?

In addition to coaching the team through a project way of working, they may need to present or train the team in one of the 54 Tools and Techniques for Business Excellence. The facilitator is also the guardian of group effectiveness in terms of how well they are managing the interplay of Content, Interaction and Process. This dynamic is summarised here and described in more detail on pages 215-216 of *54 Tools and Techniques for Business Excellence*.

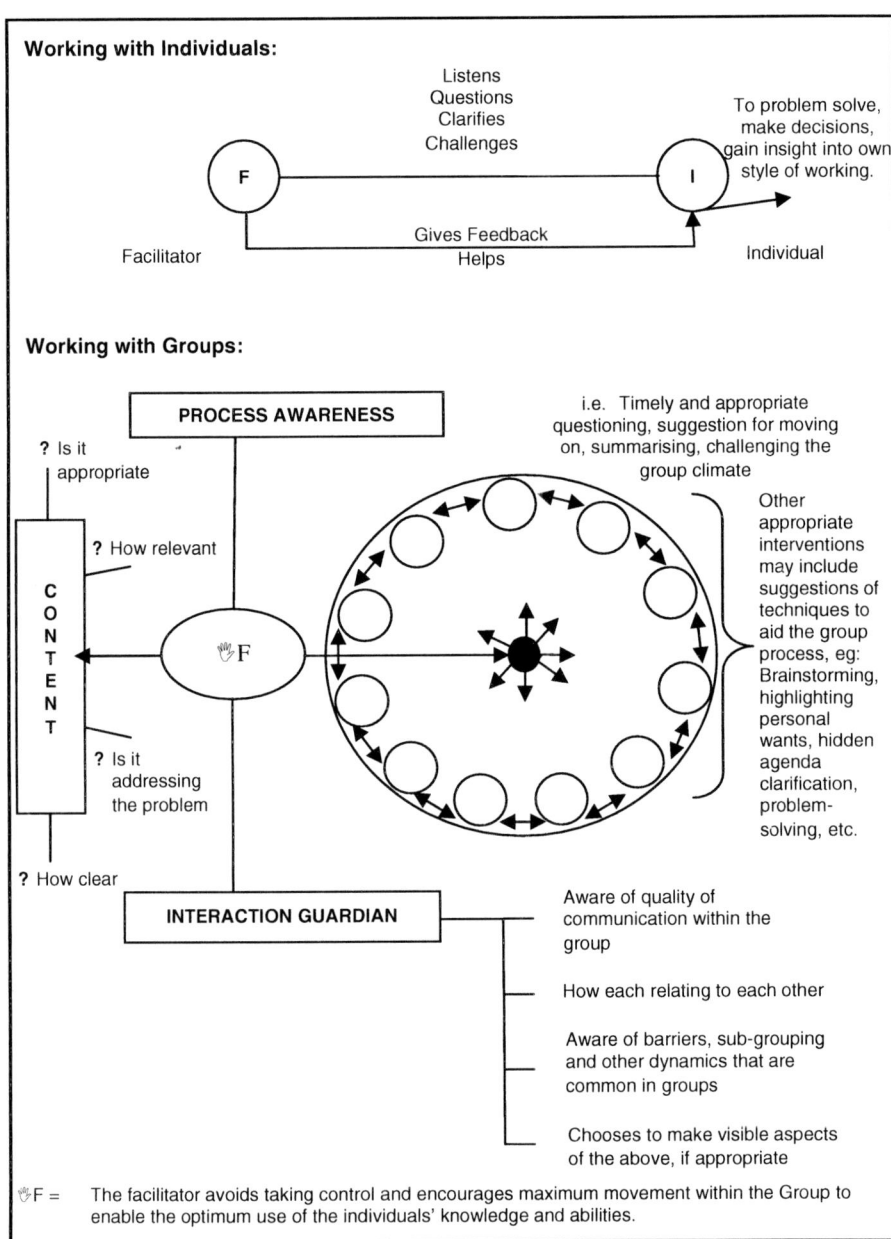

Figure 8. The process of facilitation

Facilitating groups

Contracting

One of the most significant challenges in working with a group is in ensuring that everyone understands what is expected of them in a meeting – at the outset, during, and following. It is therefore critical to establish agreement before starting the session to a number of simple but key points:

- Aims of the workshop/meeting.
- Outcomes and individual action expected.
- Method to be used in the meeting.
- Set ground rules (e.g. confidentiality, full participation, open, honest, etc.).
- Time contracted.
- Follow-up support.
- Responsibilities and roles.

The desire to make progress sometimes makes it difficult to get enough time to do this essential piece of planning work. If some of this can be completed before the workshop it will help make the best use of time when the group meets.

Managing group process

The contracting work should set the workshop up for success by giving individuals the ability to take responsibility for managing their own contributions. It is likely however that some additional management will need to be applied to the group work. I would like to offer here a simple and effective approach to working with the group process.

It uses three basic features to understand what happens between people when they work with each other:

- *Content*
  This covers the content of what is being discussed and why. It ranges from concrete data and facts to ideas and theories of what should be. It deals with imagination and direct personal experience.

- *Interaction*
  This covers the interaction between people. It ranges from giving thoughts and suggestions, speaking out and having the courage to say what is really felt, to listening to, exploring, and supporting other people.

- *Process*
  This covers the way in which a group manages its work. It ranges from setting aims and stepping forward to reach a conclusion to looking back and recalling and reviewing where they have been.

For a facilitator to manage group process effectively, it is necessary to stay in touch with all three of these elements at all times and ensure an appropriate balance, i.e.

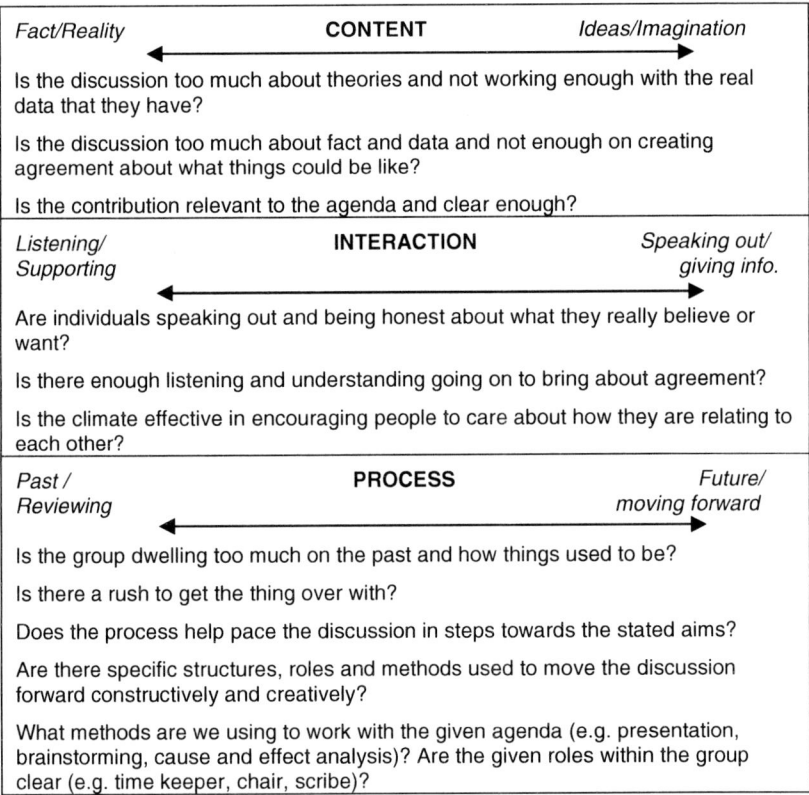

Fact/Reality	**CONTENT**	Ideas/Imagination

Is the discussion too much about theories and not working enough with the real data that they have?

Is the discussion too much about fact and data and not enough on creating agreement about what things could be like?

Is the contribution relevant to the agenda and clear enough?

Listening/ Supporting	**INTERACTION**	Speaking out/ giving info.

Are individuals speaking out and being honest about what they really believe or want?

Is there enough listening and understanding going on to bring about agreement?

Is the climate effective in encouraging people to care about how they are relating to each other?

Past / Reviewing	**PROCESS**	Future/ moving forward

Is the group dwelling too much on the past and how things used to be?

Is there a rush to get the thing over with?

Does the process help pace the discussion in steps towards the stated aims?

Are there specific structures, roles and methods used to move the discussion forward constructively and creatively?

What methods are we using to work with the given agenda (e.g. presentation, brainstorming, cause and effect analysis)? Are the given roles within the group clear (e.g. time keeper, chair, scribe)?

Review of meeting

At the end of every meeting, a legitimate role for the facilitator is to help the team express their thoughts about what went well and what could be improved in the way the meeting was managed and how everyone played their part. Smart facilitators can do this creatively and in a non threatening way.

The Role of the facilitator – a reminder of some Do's and Don'ts

Facilitators will:
- Help the project leader think through the early stage of a project.
- Help the project leader select his/her project team (by helping him/her think through criteria).
- Help the project leader design and prepare project team meetings.
- Lead the review of *any* meeting asking how it could be improved.
- Explain how a Project Management approach can help.
- Train the project team in methods to help them through the Five Stage approach. (See page 142)
- Help the project team establish ground rules of how to work together.
- Continuously reinforce the importance of Organisational Healing Values.
- Advise on the preparation needed for successful meetings.
- Develop and promote the tools and techniques for continuous improvement.
- Promote the use of Project Way of Working and effective problem-solving. (See page 142.)

Facilitators should not:
- Lead projects. (If a facilitator was nominated as a project leader, another facilitator should be identified.)
- Do the work for the project leader.
- Choose the project team.
- Chair the project meetings.
- Take minutes in meetings.
- Do the fetching and carrying for the meetings.
- Give advice or provide solutions.
- Take on tasks to deliver aspects of the projects.

The power of facilitation lay in the nature, style and timing of questions asked. Facilitation is often seen as a process of empowerment, enabling the individual or group to move on and increase confidence in the quest for improvement. The skills of facilitation are not just reserved for project team meetings but for any interaction within the context of the healing organisation, 1:1 or otherwise.

The following series of questions characterise the role and value in shaping the way teams begin to work more consistently with the vision and values of the healing organisation – essentially, raising their awareness of how effective they are in listening and responding to each other, and establishing to what extent are they getting down to the real issues.

Questions that facilitators ask

(adapted and taken from a variety of sources: see *54 Tools and Techniques for Business Excellence*, page 260)

Climate and culture setting for project teams or work groups

- How would you like the seating arranged? How do we want to work in the group?
- What roles do you want to cover (facilitator, recorder, time-keeper)? Who would like to take the role of (recorder, timekeeper)?
- What ground rules would you like? Any suggestions?
- What values are important?
- What are the characteristics of your ideal group?
- What do you not want to see happen in this group?
- If you were to be in this group for the next two years, what would you like in place now – processes, rules, guidelines?
- Is this group discussion to be confidential to the group? Any exceptions?
- Is trust important in the group? How can we develop trust?
- What are your hopes and fears regarding the group?

Managing time within a meeting or workshop

- This session will end at (time). Is everyone in agreement with this? Anyone not?
- The breaks will be at . . . and . . . Any problems with these times?
- Let's put times beside the agenda items.
- How much time will we spend on this issue?
- How much more time do you propose.
- Does everyone agree?
- Not all of the group wants to extend the discussion so we will stay with the original time agreed.

Getting participation in a group

- Let's see what everyone is thinking (or feeling). How about people who haven't spoken so far? What do you think (or feel)?
- What do you think, Sheila?
- What are your feelings about this, Christine?
- Let's have a brainstorm. Call out your ideas. Don't censor them. Barbara, could you please write the ideas on the whiteboard?
- Who'd like to speak first?
- Share with your neighbour (the person next to you).

- Who would like to share with the whole group?
- Now let's go around the whole group. We'll start here.
- Remember it's OK to pass or decline.
- Who can sum up the (issue/main ideas/areas of difference/where we have gotten to)?

Awareness of issues and dynamics

- Does anyone have anything they would like to say?
- Is anything getting in the way of anyone participating fully in this discussion?
- Is anything going on for you, Caren? You have become very quiet/look worried/seem upset. Is there anything you would like to say?
- Share with the person next to you any concerns you have about this issue.
- Is there anything you would like to share with the group?
- Are there any concerns about the group or the process?
- The energy is low. Often this indicates there are things that people are holding back. Does anyone have anything they would like to say?
- Find someone you feel comfortable with and share something you have been afraid to say in the whole group.
- Let's stand up and stretch (swap seats or do an energising exercise) to get the energy moving.
- What would it take to wake everyone up? Any suggestions?

Creating a future, vision building, clarifying outcomes

- What are your hopes and dreams about this?
- What can you see developing out of this in the future?
- What will this lead to in three years' time?
- Imagine yourself in the future (say three years from now). What do you see?
- Let's do a group visualisation exercise and see what's in the future.
- Let's pretend we have been travelling in space and arrive back to find that three years have passed. What do you see?
- What are we building?
- What do you want to end up with (or put in place)?
- What do you want to achieve?
- What outcomes are important to you?

Drawing out issues

- What are the issues here? I'll write them on the whiteboard.
- There are several issues within this discussion. Let's draw them out and address them one at a time.

- Would someone like to play the role of devil's advocate?
- There seems to be an underlying issue here which we are missing. Can anyone identify it?
- How do these issues fit together? Can someone sketch out the links on the board?
- What is the key issue here?
- These are important issues – let's list and park them so they are not lost and come back to them later.

Keeping on task

- We are getting distracted. Let's get back on task.
- Can anyone summarise where we have got to?
- How can we move this issue forward?
- What is the main task?
- What steps can we take?
- Let's put this new issue on the agenda for later and get back to the first issue.
- Who will take responsibility for carrying out this task?
- When will it be done?
- There are a lot of distractions happening – let's get back to the issue/task.
- What do we need to consider or take into account to have this resolved?

Shifting levels of group energy or attention

- How are people feeling about this issue now?
- How is the energy level?
- Who has a sense of what is going on in the group?
- Is everyone comfortable or do we need a stretch (or a break)?
- What do you think about this issue? Let's set up a continuum to get a picture of the range of views. 1 is negative, 10 is positive.
- Let's raise the energy of the group by using this technique.
- Some people have become very quiet. Can you tell us what is going on for you?
- This sounds very rational. What do people feel about it?
- This sounds very emotional. What do people think about it?

Cutting through patterned behaviour

- You have said what you don't want to happen, Matthew. Can you tell us what you would like to happen?
- Can you propose an alternative, Thomas?
- This conversation is going around in circles. Let's have a proposal we can work on.

- You have made a number of criticisms, Oliver. What has tripped you up? What has come up for you?
- What is your bottom-line concern, Dylan?
- Claire, you have had time to put forth your view. Let's hear from someone else.
- Please don't interrupt when Laura is speaking.
- Can we have one conversation at a time?
- Let's role-play to work on this issue.
- Let's separate the person from the issue.

What's not being said

- I sense that there is something here that is not being said. What is it?
- There is something going on under the surface. Can someone say what it is?
- Philippa, I sense you are holding back. What do you really want to say?
- The unsaid is louder here than the spoken.
- There seems to be a lot people are not saying.
- Who can say what's missing here?
- Let's have a round on what's missing in this discussion.
- How do you account for the (low energy/anger/lack of participation/etc.) in the group? What does it suggest to you?
- What do you think is happening here?

Identifying agreement and disagreement

- Can someone sum up the agreement already reached? Now we'll check that out with the whole group.
- The agreement we seem to have reached is . . . . Does everyone agree? The areas of disagreement are: (a) . . . . (b) . . . . (c) . . . .
- The areas of disagreement are: (a) . . . . (b) . . . . (c) . . . . Is this how everyone sees it?
- Does this wording (on the board) capture the agreement reached?
- We do not have agreement. Let's capture the different perspectives on the whiteboard.
- Can you or someone else summarise your perspective?
- Who is not happy with this solution? How do you feel, Elisha?
- What would you like changed, Thomas?
- What words would you like added or deleted?
- Please say "yes" if you agree, "no" if you don't.
- I take it that everyone agrees? (Silence means assent?)
- Can you live with this decision?
- Thank you for allowing this decision to be reached without using a veto. Would you like your contrary view written down in the records?

Learning

- What did you notice?
- Were there any surprises?
- How does this connect with what you already understand?
- How will you use these ideas?
- If you did this again, what would you like to be different?
- What have you learnt from this (project/workshop/meeting)?
- What, in essence, have you learnt – in one sentence?
- What is your learning focus now – state it in terms of 'How can I . . . . ?'

Feedback and acknowledgment

- Let's have some feedback on that idea.
- Is there any further constructive criticism?
- Now let's have positive feedback and acknowledgment.
- Let's have a round of acknowledgment.
- Find someone in the group whose work you appreciate, and go and acknowledge him or her now. Write down the names of three people in the group you admire and what it is you appreciate about them.
- We will write the feedback on the whiteboard in two columns: Constructive criticism/Acknowledgment. Let's have two rounds – the first on constructive criticism and the next on acknowledgment.

Completion

- What do you need to say to be complete on this?
- What do you need to say so that you can move on?
- What would you say now if you were never able to be with this group again?
- What would complete this for you?
- What is stopping you from being satisfied with the outcome?
- Is there anything more you need to say or do?

In addition to these group process interventions, the facilitator may be called upon to train the team in a range of techniques to enable them to manage a project or issue more effectively. The following list highlights some important techniques a facilitator will need to apply, depending on need. It is useful at the start of any facilitator training to take an audit of what they already know.

Facilitation skills and knowledge – self audit

	1 Very little experience if any	2 Know what you mean but under confident	3 Have had experience with mixed results	4 OK Reasonably Confident	5 A strength & happy with my ability
Category: Foundation Skills					
Listening					
Clarifying					
Empathy					
Questioning					
Summarising					
Self Awareness, i.e. good insight into own strengths and weaknesses					
Category: Find out what's really going on					
Cause and Effect					
Conflict Management					
Data Gathering and Display					
Ladder of Inference					
Questionnaires					
Stakeholder Analysis					
SWOT and PESTLE Analysis					
Why, why, why?					
Category: Be Focused, Prioritise					
Department Purpose Analysis (DPA)					
KIDS					
Mission Statements					
Negotiation Skills					
Pareto Analysis					
Category: Better Project Management					
Action Plans					
Cost Benefit Analysis					
Critical Path Analysis and Flowcharting					
Forcefield Analysis					
Goal Setting					
Line Graphs					
Problem Management/Solving					
Process Analysis and redesign					
Project Way of Working					
Project Control – step by step, meeting by meeting					
Solution Effect Analysis					
Category: Being the Best – Quality and Excellence					
Benchmarking					
Cost of Quality					

	1 Very little experience if any	2 Know what you mean but under confident	3 Have had experience with mixed results	4 OK Reasonably Confident	5 A strength & happy with my ability
Customer/Supplier Relationships (Internal)					
Training design and delivery					
Values Rating Exercise for Business Excellence					
Vision setting					
Workshop Design and Facilitation					
Category: Work Smarter					
Checklists					
Contingency Planning (Risk Management)					
Contracting					
Decision Analysis					
Delegation skills					
Email Management					
Presentation Skills					
Time Management					
Category: Creative Techniques					
Brainstorming					
Creative and Lateral Thinking					
Rich Picturing					
Category: People Involvement					
Career Counselling for Managers					
Challenging Skills					
Coaching, Mentoring and Action Learning					
Feedback					
Johari Window					
Leadership Styles					
Personal Development Planning					
Category: Teamwork					
Managing Groups and Teams					
Meetings – Effective meeting design and management					
Quality Action Teams					
Category: Total Organisational Change					
Culture Change					
Organisation Development Process					
How Organisations Develop					
Understanding how the Shadow Side of organisations influence people and decisions					
The meaning of Strategy in context of organisation vision					

> **26. Nurture an internal network of facilitators utilising the structures Action Learning has to offer.**

The ongoing development of facilitators and action learning

Facilitator training is the start of a journey which needs support and stimulus. This support can be designed in a way that serves the business and adds momentum to the healing organisation process.

This is achieved by creating a network of Action Learning Sets.

Action Learning, first described by Reg Revens in his book, *ABC of Action Learning*,[6] is a deceptively simple but powerful process.

In summary, action learning brings together small groups of participants with the following intentions:

- To work on and through organisational/individual issues. This is most effective when the commitment is *voluntary*.
- To work on real problems. Situations in which *"I am part of the problem and the problem is part of me"* although this may take some time to realise.
- To work together to check individual perceptions, clarify (and render more manageable) the issue and explore alternatives for action. Using the processes and skills learned during facilitator training.
- To take action in the light of new insight. Begin to change the situation.
- Bring an account of the consequences back to the group for further shared reflection. Updating on degree of success but more importantly, what the individual has learned about themselves.
- To be aware of group processes and develop effective ways of working together. Understanding the dynamics of the set and how each individual is influencing the group experience.
- To provide the balance of support and challenge that enables each person to manage themselves and others more effectively. Thus increasing confidence to re-engage with the organisation.

Each action learning set (usually made up of between 4 to 7 members) is supported by a trained ALS facilitator, sometimes referred to as a change agent or coordinator.

---

[6] Revans, R., *ABC of Action Learning*, Lemos & Crane (UK), 1998

To enable the learning network to thrive, an organisation needs to identify highly competent managers to be 'change agents', i.e. to lead and supervise the facilitators and become the eyes and ears of 'change'. By training these agents in Action Learning Set facilitator skills, they then can, on a regular basis, not only support the development of facilitators, but also listen in and report back to a 'steering group' the reality of the process of change. This report back needs to be issue based and not personal based, thus respecting the confidentiality of Action Learning Sets.

This learning network is summarised in Figure 9 and Figure 10.

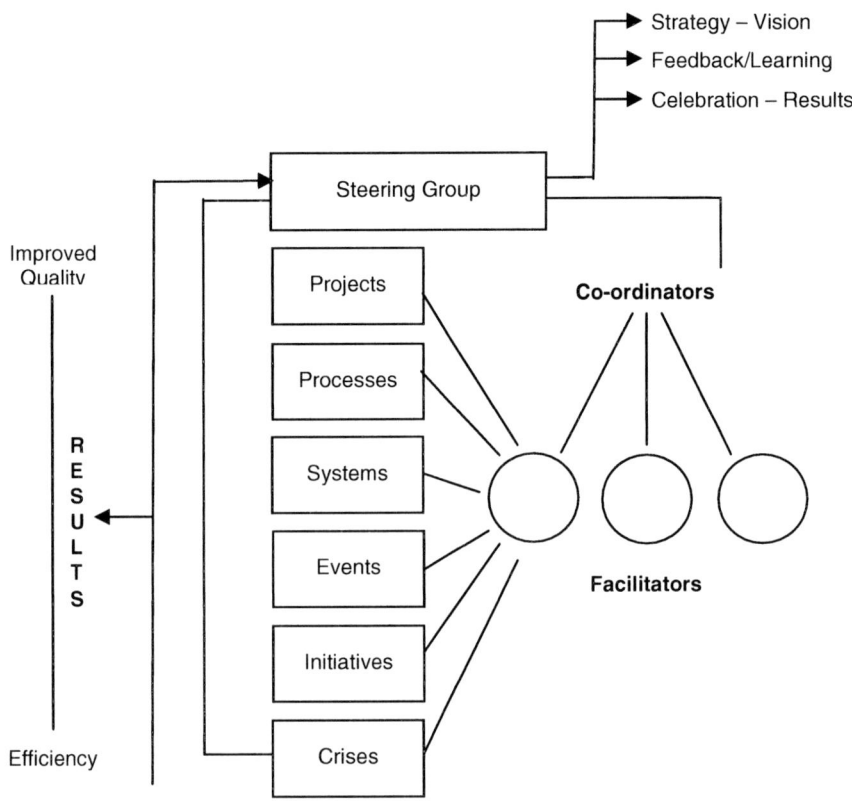

Figure 9. Networking co-ordinators and facilitators

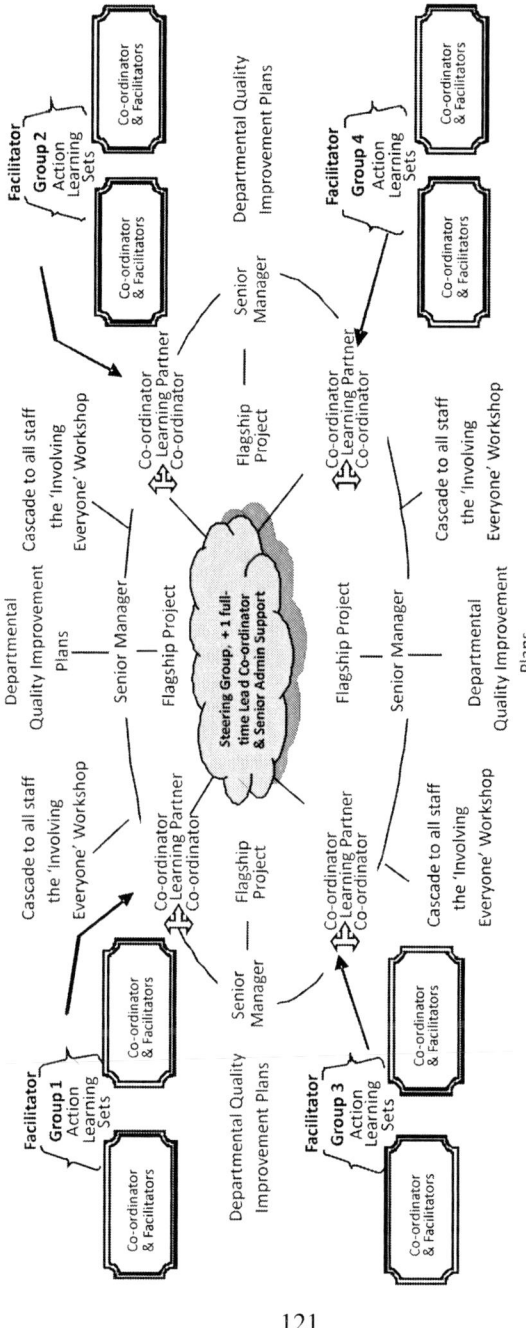

Figure 10. The learning network – creating a healing culture from within

The learning environment created in Action Learning Sets needs to be characteristic and consistent with healing organisation values and will require agreed and contracted ground rules, i.e.

- Open.
- Honest.
- Confidential.
- Take a risk – it's OK to make mistakes.
- Encourage participation.
- Listen and respect.
- Challenge with understanding.
- Commitment – time (usually at least once a month – 6 people can take at least ½ a day, sometimes a full day).

The learning set works at a number of different levels:

- The problem presented – operationally based, a will to change/improve it, clear responsibility for doing so lays with the member.

- Self development – seeking opportunity for feedback and challenge. Learning more about self by others sharing their perspective and skilfully helping the participant recognise their contribution to the problem, and hence the solution.

- Facilitator/Leadership skill development – each participant encouraged to practise the interpersonal skills, processes and techniques that they will need to become proficient in. In doing so, taking a risk, making mistakes and providing further opportunities for learning.

- Group awareness – raising sensitivity and skill in handling complex dynamics within a group problem-solving situation. Recognising how the balance and interplay of Content, Interaction and Process (see page 109) are important in shaping the development of the group discussion.

- Organisational insight – recognising themes and connections can help focus on shared issues with a collective will to work together and influence thus making a significant contribution to achieving healing organisation status.

To achieve this creative and intensive learning experience, the Action Learning Set facilitator needs to be highly skilled and confident, versed with the full range of interpersonal and group skills to ensure there is an appropriate balance between coaching, strong facilitation and light touch facilitation. In addition to these general skills, I use several creative techniques.

Fly on the wall

The group listening to the story asks questions for clarification; then, after about 15 minutes, the story-teller is asked to sit outside the group and listen in while the rest of the group review the story, share their perceptions, highlight confusion and ask further questions. After, say, 10 minutes of this review, the participant is invited back into the group to express the thoughts and feelings they had while listening to the review.

Rarely do you get an opportunity to hear what other people's perceptions are of you and your situation in an open environment. This process frees the group up and at the same time enables the individual to have some valuable reflection time.

A picture paints a thousand words

While the individual tells their story, each group member sketches, using cartoon, symbols and pictures, an impression of what they think the key elements or issues contained in the story are.

The group then, in turn, use their pictures to summarise their perception of what they have heard. When everyone has done this, the storyteller gives feedback as to what was useful, relevant, insightful or otherwise.

A challenging question

It is important to establish the principle of 'earning the right to challenge' by demonstrating empathy first. However, after a while the Action Learning Set facilitator may judge that a number of challenges are required. To free this opportunity up, each participant is asked to write down a challenging question to the story-teller.

Then, in turn, they read out their challenges while the storyteller takes notes in preparation for responding. The response needs to be in the order of what they felt was 'useful, helpful and most challenging because . . . .'

These are just three specific techniques I use, combined with role play, use of metaphors, direct input of theory and sharing personal experience.

Any healing organisation will need a living, thriving and growing network of Action Learning.

Reg Revens states that organisations (and those within them) cannot survive or flourish unless the rate of learning is equal to or greater than the rate of change they are experiencing.

Many of the organisations I work with (e.g. Health Service, Education and Airlines) are forever playing catch-up – the pace of change seems to be greater than the pace of learning – hence the importance of making a significant investment in the structures and processes of learning.

Once facilitators are an accepted and valued role in the organisation, it will become self-evident that these facilitation skills are essential management skills and it therefore makes sense to integrate the nature of facilitator development into the organisations leadership development programme.

> **27. Ensure the opportunity for learning is greater than or equal to the pace of change.**

Facilitators, through action learning, create support for themselves, at the same time, gain real insight to organisational problems. They can directly improve the efficiency of the organisation by attacking directly the cost of failure.

The cost of quality and failure

So far, the importance of developing the Board and executive team has been stressed. This development, alongside the training of facilitators to support the organisation wide improvement process is crucial groundwork before launching into asking for everyone's involvement in the process of improvement.

In Chapter 3, Dave Battle's request for everyone's cooperation backfired as he was dealing with a resistant and cynical workforce. He now realises there is a lot more to engaging everyone in the organisation and he can't do it on his own.

Firstly, he needs his own team to share with him the commitment and excitement associated with the vision. Then a process for cascading vision, values and clarity as to how people can get involved needs to be designed and supported by competent facilitators.

A key element underpinning all this is to change the 'blame culture' into a learning culture.

As illustrated in our story, the blame culture is alive and well in the Delectrex top team and as yet there is little sign of an approach that can review what is happening in an objective and rational way.

It is important that changing from 'no blame' to a positive review/learning opportunity does not detract from the importance of accountability.

Some say a 'fair blame' culture is appropriate.

I disagree, as the emphasis in this approach is still on the individual or group, rather than choosing the opportunity for learning and putting in preventative measures for the future.

Clarity about who is accountable should be part of this but not the focus. The people accountable could also be the people who may benefit most from a positive review (with clear development needs identified and ongoing support for improvement contracted).

Any failing in an organisation should be reviewed with the intention of learning from it and, consequently, putting in prevention and improvement steps. Rarely is one individual entirely to blame for organisational mistakes and failure. It is more likely to be a combination of errors by a number of individuals within the context of unclear communication, policy or inappropriate procedures or systems. The total picture needs to be considered in an atmosphere of positive review and commitment for making improvement recommendation that go beyond personal development of the individuals concerned. So often, reviews stop short of understanding the immediate cause and effect. A more challenging question is to ask how the situation occurred in the first place, perhaps utilising the "Why, Why, Why?" technique (as described in *54 Tools and Techniques for Business Excellence,* Technique N° 8, page 38) to get a deeper understanding of what can be a range of complex and deep seated factors associated with incidents occurring. This is likely to involve identifying the 'governing values' as described in the concept of double loop learning (See page 201).

The concept of failure is not one that rests easily with successful leaders. They are more likely to reframe 'failure' to 'setback', or 'opportunity for improvement'. However, there is a concept of failure that can be extremely useful, especially if everyone in the organisation understood and appreciated it. This is the concept of 'failure' associated with 'quality'.

The definition of quality failure simply means anything that goes wrong in the organisation that could have been prevented and takes time to put right is a 'failure cost', i.e. it takes time to put it right and therefore is a cost to the organisation. This failure cost is one element within the 'cost of quality'. A fuller description with examples is given here:

The price of non-conformance (Crosby, P.[7]) or the cost of poor quality (Juran, J.[8]), or, more simply, the 'cost of quality' refers to the costs associated with providing poor quality product or service.

These costs are usually conceptualised under three categories:

1. Prevention costs

Prevention Costs are those costs of all activities undertaken to *prevent* defects or failures related to the end result of either production or service.

---

[7] Crosby, P., *Quality is Free,* McGraw-Hill, 1979
[8] Juran, J.M., *Managerial Breakthrough,* McGraw Hill, 1964

2. Failure costs

Failure Costs are incurred when products or services do not meet their specification or conform to their agreed requirement. This cost *includes* every aspect of the production or provision of that service that culminates in *failure*. Therefore, every element of time, labour materials, design, management, marketing, linked to the non-conformance are failure costs related to that product or service.

3. Appraisal costs

Appraisal Costs are incurred in every aspect of inspection and planned evaluation designed to ensure that defects in the work product or service do not continue if it does not conform to requirements. Usually, *appraisal* is accompanied by appropriate documentation, which takes time to complete and compile, as do the development of specification for appraisal, and the organisation of re-work to modify defects. In other words, formal checks to ensure service or product meets the required standard.

Examples of prevention, appraisal and failure costs

Prevention costs

Take the aspects from creation of a service or "product" through to the delivery of the service or "product" to the end-user. For example, start and follow through all steps in the process of a patient care pathway or from customer order to delivery.

Often the steps from "Creation" to "Delivery" involve a person or persons in line, each of whom is dependent on the previous person in the line, i.e. internal and external customer/supplier connections.

Prevention costs are those costs of all activities undertaken to prevent defects, mistakes or complications related to the end result, thus ensuring the end result is right first time.

Examples include:

- Mission, role, clear customer requirements, objective setting, training, education.
- Reviews, to learn how to improve. Effective problem-solving.
- Forward planning, clear priorities, accurate forecasts and resource allocation.

Failure costs

These are costs associated with items which failed to meet or conform to the agreed requirements. These costs include all material and people involved.

Costs can include the internal organisational costs as well as those related to lost productivity.

Examples include:
- Chasing reports, notes or results
- Misreading data
- Slow transport system
- Inappropriate use of email
- Meetings starting and finishing late
- System failure
- Inadequate or inappropriate training

Appraisal costs

These are costs incurred conducting inspections and planned evaluations to determine whether the work product or support service/general service conforms to the requirements.

Documents which describe the conformance required are relevant. This includes specifications, briefs etc.

Examples include:
- Monitoring, evaluating, checking against standards
- Proof reading
- Audits and inspection
- Check lists indicating fulfilment of contract
- Appraisals if measured against competencies or standards/norms

Managing the cost of quality

Reducing the cost of quality is one of the principal targets in organisation improvement. If an organisation is draining itself with waste, eventually the cost consequences will make 'healing' very difficult.

Reduction in failure costs and the gradual decrease in the need to rely on heavy appraisal costs constitute some of the most significant financial benefits of improvement. A small increase in prevention costs can create a massive reduction in failure costs. See Figure 11, page 129.

The success of quality cost containment relies on each individual within the organisation being fully aware of the impact they have on the customer/supplier chain, and how the effect of sub-standard work reverberates around the chain, incurring obvious and less obvious costs as time and materials are wasted, work patterns are disrupted, and re-work is undertaken.

The key to understanding the above is clear knowledge of who the customer is, both externally and internally, and aiming to exceed their expectation by delivering this excellence. The development of this knowledge implies increased communication and cross functional problem-solving, which includes customer and supplier.

Each person, then, must develop a concern for excellence, and constantly strive for 'right first time, every time'. To do this, individual effort in this direction *must* be given adequate recognition, opportunity and authority to change systems, etc. This can be achieved with the support of facilitation and the implementation of Quality Action Teams (page 152).

Imagine everyone in the organisation understanding the concept of 'cost of quality' and applying this concept to recognising and highlighting the failures that occur within their own sphere of control. Imagine next, everyone having the support and opportunity to act on these failures – each person having the facility to heal their own situation – following through, creating a healthier and more productive work environment.

This is possible if, once the investment in Board, executive team development and facilitator training is made, plans to cascade these concepts to everyone in the organisation can be made. The nature of the cascade has to be totally inclusive, engaging and creative, with positive role models at the top of the organisation becoming clearly visible. Details about the cascade process and the structures used to encourage staff to work together on improvement initiatives are described later.

This element of 'ownership' highlights the importance of understanding why the organisation needs to change. This understanding then needs cascading throughout the organisation with conviction and passion demonstrated through the behaviour of the Board and Executive team.

This cascade of understanding is aided by a team of trained facilitators who help raise awareness (Chapter 1, page 18) of how people can improve the way they work together and in particular how to reduce the cost of failure they are directly involved with and hence own.

Imagine everyone taking responsibility to improve five things they do each day – the challenge then is how to sustain this momentum of healing at every level. A certain degree of confidence and belief in your manager and fellow co-workers will be needed. More importantly an opportunity for everyone to believe in themselves. Communicating this opportunity genuinely with passion is a challenge explored in the next chapter.

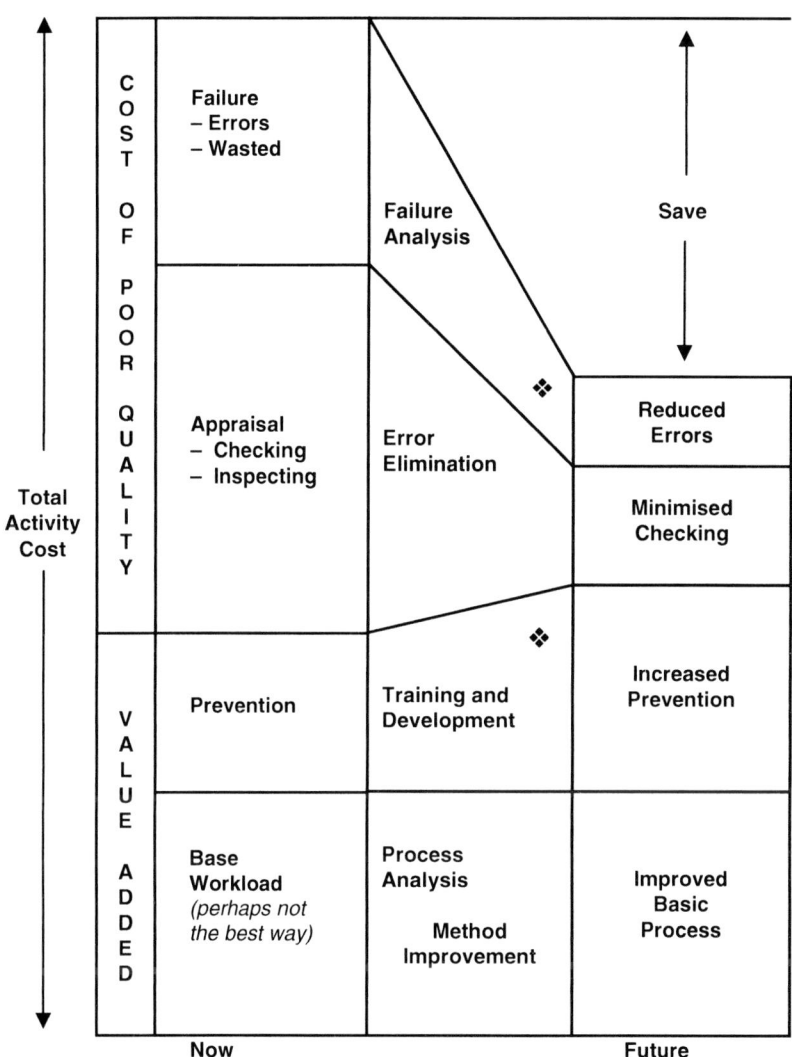

Figure 11. The cost of quality

28. Engage everyone in identifying the failure costs in the organisation. Use Pareto and identify the important 20% and apply the new ways of working to put them right, thus achieving significant cost improvement.

5

Belief

The power of faith healing is well documented. This phenomenon seems to indicate incredible ability to influence positive forces within ourselves to counter the negative.

Cancerous tumours have been known to shrink or to disappear from patients who have refused conventional treatment and opted for more eastern, meditative and homeopathic remedies. There have been cases where conventional treatment has failed yet the power of self-belief has prevailed. A will to live, a belief that it is possible, combined with the ability to visualise the battles being won, results in what is often perceived as a miraculous cure. People given a prognosis of "months to live" can live on for years with a belief and a will to make it happen.

Having faith and belief in what the organisation is trying to do, having a clear vision as to what is possible and the motivation to commit to achieving this vision, will give each individual hope and a sense of optimism for the future. A self-fulfilling prophecy of success, with a positive outlook as to how this is to be achieved, are significant contributing factors to the process of organisational healing.

However, having faith alone may not be sufficient. Can Dave Battle capitalise on the good foundation work achieved so far and follow through with effective and practical support methods and techniques?

Delectrex Limited

You could cut the atmosphere with a knife. The group had been warmed up. It had been an uneasy start, but the two facilitators – Myles the IT manager and Sheila the once cynical (now facilitator) shift leader – did a good job in encouraging the group to introduce themselves in terms of how they related to customers.

It was fun and insightful, especially when everyone stood back and commented on the complex web of connections everyone had in terms of being each other's customers and suppliers.

The anticipation now was a curious combination of cynicism and excitement.

These workshops were beginning to create a positive ripple of hope and enthusiasm. However, since Dave Battle's last effort of 'motivating the troops' had been such a fiasco, the jury was still out!

Dave cleared his throat. No jacket, sleeves rolled up, he perched on the edge of the desk. He had no notes or presentation slides . . . .

"First of all, thanks for coming and participating in what, I believe, is one of the most exciting developments our company has ever known. I choose my words carefully, I do believe it is *our* company. It belongs to you and me and we all have an opportunity to work together and turn it from a good company to a great company. I have always been ambitious, not just for status and wealth, but more importantly to make a difference. When I got this job, I was delighted, because I now had an opportunity to make that difference. However, I quickly realised that I couldn't do this on my own and I needed help. I need help from you and that's why we are here today – together!"

Dave had got their attention and this was different. He stood up and walked to the window, glanced outside to a typical overcast sky, then turned to his audience.

"So, what's the difference I want to make? I want to change this company from a good company to a great company. One where we can be really proud of what we do, one where we get excited to come to work, one where we have fun, create new ideas, and get great satisfaction from delighting our customers. It's not just about producing wiring harnesses and tools for the motor trade – it's doing it in such a way that creates efficient, safe and greener motoring – there is a bigger picture. If we achieve this, then we grow, we become more secure, we create more opportunities for advancement and we create a happy, healthy working environment where we learn and thrive with confidence."

Dave's voice had an emotional tone about it. He spoke from the heart, but one or two frowns appeared on the faces of his captive audience.

"OK, what does this mean in reality? How are we going to do it?" Dave described the programme of organisation-wide improvement he had in mind. He called it 'Quality Through Leadership'. He explained the concept, giving it an identity, a brand so they could communicate consistently to everyone exactly what 'Quality Through Leadership' meant.

"Hands up all those who are leaders?"

One or two of the more senior managers of this mixed-level cross section of people from the company sheepishly put their hands up.

"Wrong! You are ALL leaders. 'Quality Through Leadership' means we are all responsible for the quality of our work. Leadership is about taking the initiative to improve the work we do. So, hands up who wants to improve what they do?"

Everyone puts their hand up. "That's leadership!"

Dave went on and talked about future company challenges and opportunities, then paused for one or two questions. On parting, he said "Thanks again, everyone. I will just leave you with a story about building cathedrals." Dave illustrated the difference between the stone-cutter and the cathedral builder (page 70) using the local city's Cathedral – he paused and thanked them all again.

This time, the round of applause given was genuine and heartfelt.

* * * * *

"OK, everyone. I have a summary of the Pareto failure activities so far." Daphne confidently stands up to present to the 'Quality Through Leadership' steering group, made up of the executive team, Organisational Development programme Manager, two facilitators and the non-executive Champion, Mavis, who in her previous job had been the Director of Organisation Development for a large retail company.

"We have run 60 workshops so far, and have about 60 more to do, but it looks clear what the main problems are:

- poor communication, in particular
  - inappropriate and over use of email
  - too many, and badly managed, meetings
- lack of IT support
  - system failures
  - technical problems
  - delays in updating software
- customer complaints
  - wrong order fulfilment
  - delays in delivery."

Daphne continues. She is quite pleased with the task of taking the output of each workshop. The list of brainstormed failure activities is an overwhelming case for major investment in communication, training, re-design of processes and dedication to creating a healing, healthy, continuously improving culture.

"OK!" Dan begins to summarise.

In an ingenious moment of insight, at the golf club with his friend and playing partner Ged Shaw, Dave had realised that he would get more out of his disappointed and de-motivated Operations Director if he gave him Executive Lead responsibility for the programme. It seemed to be working.

"What we need are some 'flagship' projects. Projects that will lead the way, show how we can do things differently, putting everything that the facilitators have learnt into practice. These flagship projects should focus on our top failure activities: communication, IT and customer complaints.

"Excellent Dan. I agree!" Dave seemed to have learned better to let go and support rather than control and criticise.

Dick, the Finance Director, becomes unusually animated "You know, the savings we could make are enormous! If only we could get everyone in the organisation involved in reducing failure in this structured way."

"We can!" Alison, the Programme Manager, jumped up and explained how the cascade of workshops progress into supporting 'Quality Action Teams' involving everyone in the pursuit of reducing failure, improving efficiency and quality.

*   *   *   *   *

"Wow Dave, you have well and truly thrashed me today!"

"A few holes to go yet, Ged. Come on, it's not like you to give up!"

"I'm just acknowledging how well you're playing. What's different?"

Dave strides on after hitting a perfect five iron shot 165 yards to land softly on the green, one metre from the hole. "I guess when your heart and your head are together, your game comes together!"

"That's the sort of thing I would say, Dave."

"Well, you do talk a load of bullshit sometimes, Ged, but the last few weeks our chats have helped me realise more and more that this 'game of work', like golf, is all about self-belief, positive thinking, focus, listening and responding appropriately to what's happening in the moment."

"Bloody hell, Dave! Sounds great, and you're beginning to recreate this philosophy at work?"

"Yep!" Dave lines up his putt, remembering the power of visualising the line, feeling the green and believing in the result you want.

The satisfying sound of the ball in the hole gives rise to a clenched fist and punch in the air.

"Yes! My hole, and game, I believe, Ged!"

It seems that Dave Battle has achieved a number of breakthroughs.

He has regained the confidence of his team, invested in training his own team of facilitators, and recruited a programme manager, Alison, who has gained consultancy support from a consultant friend of Ged Shaw's to help design and implement 'Quality Through Leadership'.

The story illustrates essential elements for successful organisational healing:

- Challenge denial ('everything is OK').
- Find the motivation, the will and the drive to survive and be successful.
- Visualise the alternative and communicate the desired future.
- Believe it is possible and recognise the personal power and potential of everyone.
- Remain positive, optimistic and continually recognise and build on the strengths and successes.

Initially, to embark upon an organisation-wide programme of healing requires an element of faith. For the more cynical who have, over the years, been part of many initiatives which have turned out to be 'flavour of the month (or year)', it will require a leap of faith.

This belief, faith, conviction and drive towards a vision to achieve a 'great organisation' can successfully be communicated in the environment of an engaging workshop. These workshops need to be designed and run by trained facilitators in the context of support and preparation from the company board and executive team as described in the previous chapter.

Once this support is in place, then good workshop design, project management and involvement of everyone in Quality Action Teams can progress. These stages are described here in this chapter, under the following:

- Cascade workshop design and delivery
- A project way of working (PWOW) for managing change
- Quality Action Teams – a step by step guide

Cascade workshop design and delivery

Who, when, how long?

Once the decision has been made to involve everyone, and following facilitator training, plans can then be made to deliver workshops to everyone. This will involve careful logistical design and preparation.

A quick calculation based on a workshop size of 12 to 15 participants will give an indication of the scale and scope of the exercise. In our fictitious organisation, Delectrex Limited, there are 2000 staff. This will require approximately 120 half day workshops. However, it's important to consider whether the middle managers and specialist/professional groups need more time. This is because not only will they have to accept and own the proposition of a 'healing organisation'; they will also have to contribute to creating the environment and opportunity for their staff to be involved. Therefore, they will need to understand the importance of coaching and demonstrate the leadership skills associated with the organisational values expressed.

So, in a company the size of Delectrex Limited they will need four one-day workshops for their 60 managers and 120 half-day workshops for the rest of their staff.

When embarking upon such an exercise, ideally you want everyone willing to come with an open mind. However, the reality is that a fair proportion of the staff will react by claiming they have better things to do with their time and ask whether the workshops are mandatory.

---

29. The more you communicate your belief about what's possible with conviction and passion, the more prepared your staff are to take a leap of faith. Especially if this communication is supported by appropriate decisions and behaviours.

The invitation letter to attend needs to come from the Chief Executive/Managing Director and should be worded in such a way that it would be very 'difficult' to refuse the invitation.

This is a copy of the letter Dave Battle sent:

Dear _____

A place has been reserved for you at a 'Quality through Leadership' workshop. Every member of staff will be attending a workshop over the next three months. It will take half a day and you will need to contact Alison on Extension 5454 or email her to confirm your morning or afternoon slot.

Your Workshop Date is: _____

am: 9.00 – 13.00/ pm: 13.30 – 17.00

This is an important, critical and exciting opportunity for you to be directly involved in the future development of our Company.

We have plans to grow and build on our success and we need your support, help and involvement to progress our plans.

I, or one of the executive team, will attend to let you know what we are planning.

If you have any difficulties or problems with this invitation, please talk to Alison or myself. It's important we get 100% attendance.

I look forward to working with you and thank you in anticipation of your commitment and involvement.

Yours sincerely

Dave Battle

Managing Director

The tone of the letter needs to be inviting, positive, yet firm. If, after this invite, you still get a refusal or repeated excuses, then the challenge to this minority is 'fine, if you don't want to be involved, then please tell me your alternative methods for achieving our vision?' This challenge usually engenders compliance or becomes an alternative career option discussion. It is important to understand resistance and defensiveness – these are important clues as to what may thwart or sabotage proposed changes in the future.

Preparation and set-up

An exercise such as this requires almost a full-time administrative project. The administrator will need to identify rooms for workshop delivery, book places on each workshop (following a discussion as to the appropriate mix of participants), match facilitators to workshops, prepare materials, equipment and deal with the inevitable questions for clarification and enquiries and request for changes in dates, etc.

Part of the training of facilitators will involve them in preparing to run exercises to engage the rest of the staff in the programme. This engagement needs to be consistent with the desired culture (e.g. open, honest, creative, encourages participation, respectful of each other and each others' ideas, support for each other and customer focused).

Participants need not only to *hear* the message, but to *experience* it. This is the only way to get the level of emotional commitment essential for self-healing and the consequent organisational healing.

Each workshop will need facilitating by two facilitators. They will need to work together to agree roles, prepare materials and, if necessary, rehearse so that they are familiar enough to be confident in dealing with resistance, questions and challenges.

---

30. Design in quality time for all staff to be directly engaged in hearing the 'vision' and having the opportunity to contribute ideas for improvement.

The workshops will create significant demands on the time of the executive team. Over 120 workshops to be attended by an executive team member for the 'Vision' presentation session (one hour only) means that if shared equally, then each member over a period of three months will need to attend 24 workshops.

Other factors such as shift-working and time-critical jobs will also need to be considered.

Ultimately, it will be important to measure the impact of the workshops. This can be done by agreeing Key Performance Indicators, such as number of Quality Action Teams formed, or percentage of efficiency savings made.

Design and delivery

The design and delivery of the workshops need to be consistent so that everyone gets a similar experience. However, some flexibility can be built in depending on the strengths and talents of the facilitators. The range of exercises should be agreed beforehand, as should the learning outcomes. Certain elements of each workshop are critical and need to be consistent. These are:

- Vision for the organisation.
- Cost of Quality exercise to identify failure outcomes.
- Overview of 'Quality Through Leadership' (the programme).

The rest of the workshop fundamentally should be designed to encourage participation and address issues and concerns, with clarification about next steps.

> **31. Each executive team member needs to take a share in delivery of the vision personally.**

It is important to ensure consistency in the approach and style of workshop delivery. Too much variation in delivery can detract from the key messages. A typical half-day workshop design is shown in Figure 12.

TIME	TITLE	PURPOSE	PROCESS	MATERIALS/NOTES
09.00	Introduction and brief overview of the workshop Workshop Climate and Groundrules	To get to know each other in terms of how we relate as customers and suppliers. Set workshop learning environment.	Large white board/pens to write name, function & draw connecting customer/supplier lines to each other. Stand back & review significance.	Large white board or Flip Charts Whiteboard/Marker Pens
09.30	Overview of the 'Quality through Leadership' programme	To highlight the overall process, time line, investments, plans and level of commitment.	Presentation with questions and answers.	Time line, pictorial representation, handouts linking Vision, Values and Behaviours to the main strands of OD.
10.00	Vision Presentation	To clarify company direction and commitment to creating excellence.	Presentation by Chief Executive or Executive Team member. Encourage reaction/response.	May need slides/support materials (OHP/Screen) to ensure consistent message.
10.45	BREAK			Refreshments available.
11.00	Cost of Quality	To explain the concepts of Prevention, Appraisal and Failure.	Presentation and quiz to test understanding.	Handout, quiz and prize for winner.
11.30	Failure Activity Brainstorm and Pareto	To identify the top failure activities.	Explain groundrules for Brainstorm. Flip chart failure activities. Explain Pareto. Use voting system to agree groups' top list.	Plenty of flip chart paper and pens. Wall space for charts. Blue Tac.
12.15	Quality Action Teams	To understand how local improvements can be made.	Input step by step approach and explain facilitator support available.	Ensure list and contact details of facilitators available.
12.45	Review	To offer first reactions and feedback	Use a creative and positive approach, e.g. use of metaphors.	
13.00	FINISH			

Figure 12. Typical workshop design

The exercise using cost of quality concepts provides the organisation with a rolling diagnostic from every level about what the potential improvement priorities are in terms of improving efficiency and customer service.

This diagnostic, as illustrated in Delectrex Limited's steering group meeting, can be used to identify priority projects whereby approaches to working smarter, being creative and sustaining improvement consistent with the healing process are achieved.

The participants of each workshop should come away feeling positive and confident. They will have experienced 'Quality Through Leadership' in action in the way they were treated: the welcome, coffee/refreshments on arrival, the room set up professionally, inspirational posters on the wall, music in the background, all equipment ready and tested, excellent listening and coaching demonstrated by the facilitators, and so on. The facilitators will need to demonstrate effective listening in what may be a difficult experience. If there are members of the audience who are cynical, defensive, critical or even aggressive then very loaded questions may be asked. The facilitators will have had some preparation in their training to deal with awkward questions and the following list is not untypical:

1. What does a facilitator do?
2. Why change – what's wrong with what we have got?
3. How can we justify days on end training facilitators in a posh hotel – surely the money could be spent on other things?
4. What's this thing called Project Way of Working? I already know how to manage projects.
5. Are these cascade workshops compulsory? And what are they anyway?
6. I need help with a project meeting. Can you help me set it up and perhaps Chair it for me?
7. How do I set up a Quality Action Team for my staff?
8. What are these values and why are they important?
9. What does 'Quality Through Leadership' mean?
10. Why were *you* selected as a facilitator?
11. How will we know all this investment is going to be worth it?
12. Why are we doing this now, when in a few months time it's all change again with the new computer system?
13. What's the point in us changing when you see Senior Managers behaving badly or not see them at all? (They don't practise what they preach)
14. How can we involve our external suppliers?
15. I think this is all a waste of time and money – it won't make a difference, its flavour of the month – show me the evidence that this works.

Understanding what's behind the questions (what are the deeper emotions, fears and hopes) and giving non-defensive information will demonstrate that the momentum of positive healing and change is already evident and working. A key message being, 'This is the start of an ongoing journey – and now it's up to you to get involved.'

Direct involvement can occur just by individuals taking personal initiative to improve things and by getting involved in 'Quality Action Teams' (page 152) and/or 'Project Way of Working' (PWOW).

A Project Way of Working for managing change

'Prevention is better than the cure'. When applied to organisations, this means getting it right first time by spending time applying effective problem-solving and empowerment in projects for improvement.

> **32. Integrate the process of empowerment into a preventative project management approach (PWOW).**

This approach integrates a simple **five stage approach** to project 'foundation' management (this is not full project implementation or control) and the problem-solving process previously described. The integration of these can be seen in Figure 13 on page 143.

Figure 13. A project way of working (PWOW)

The application of this approach in itself is not enough. It needs to be a multi-disciplinary team activity, whereby the meetings are well managed and the experience of team members is one of stimulated, creative learning and positive contribution. Here, the trained facilitators support the project leader in chairing the meetings with an explicit joint agenda, i.e. to improve the organisation by working on the identified failure activities, *and* apply the new techniques learnt by the facilitator. Every team member gains personal benefit and ideas for applying the same techniques within their own sphere of control.

A detailed description is given here in terms of roles, responsibilities and step by step approach:

Stage one: Establishing the project

The first stage is to ensure that the project is set up to succeed. Likely tasks within this stage would be:

- Agreeing project purpose.
- Establishing sponsorship arrangements.
- Recruiting project leader. (Someone who would lead the project as part of their day-to-day job – not a full time or specialist role.)
- Recruiting project team from the key stakeholders. Agreeing roles and responsibilities.
- Agreeing project stages, timescales, and discussing project tools including systems of measurement.
- Ensuring the provision of any skills training that may be required by members of the project team.

This first stage is critical to ensure the success of the project. Clear project purpose and clear management arrangements should together provide the necessary direction.

These can be summarised on a project proposal form, designed to help consistency of approach and communication (see example form on page 145).

Stage one – Step one

Maximise our knowledge of the present situation. (**Step 1**)

What's going on? Whatever the proposal, whether it's problem orientated (e.g. 'we need to improve the way we communicate with our customer') or connected with new implementation of a policy or system, the first stage is to complete a proposal and gather initial information about the current situation. (See example form on page 145.)

Example Form   Project Proposal

Identification Name   _____

Start Date   _____

1. Initial presentation or awareness of need for change.

2. Project Sponsor   _____

3. Project Leader   _____

4. Project Team   _____

5. Initial intended outcome (to be reviewed when clear vision and goals are set)

6. Approximate timescale (to be reviewed when project scope is more definite)

7. Expected benefits

8. Initial estimate of costs and/or savings

9. Risks (Reviewing potential pitfalls and if necessary design contingency plans, see T&T No 33)

10. Key stakeholders to be included in the communication plan. Description of first steps in the communication plan. What, to whom, when and how?

Project roles and responsibilities

Each project will require leadership, management and a range of experts dependent on the needs of particular projects. As a minimum, projects should have an identified project sponsor and a project leader. There are also other roles that may be necessary but should not be obligatory.

Project sponsor

The project sponsor will be a senior manager who is best placed to champion the project. They may or may not have identified the need for the project but will certainly be very keen that the project succeeds. The project sponsor will play a lead role in conceiving and scoping the project but will be removed from planning and implementation. The project sponsor is likely to be involved in unblocking projects, supporting the management of resistance and keeping a watchful eye on progress. They will probably attend the occasional meeting of the project team but can expect regular briefings.

Project leader

The project leader will have day-to-day responsibility for the project. Their role will be to lead the project team through the five stages of project management, described in this approach of Project Way of Working (PWOW). The project leader is likely to bring in general change management and team leadership skills rather than technical skills. The project leader will report to the project sponsor for the purposes of the project.

Other roles

There may be many other possible roles which would relate to specific needs of the project. These 'experts' would be called upon as appropriate and may be able to offer skills associated with database management, process mapping, costing quality, information recording, meeting organisation and administration.

Project team

The project team will be formed by the project leader. It will be lead by the project leader and will comprise of individuals who can contribute to the project, either because of their knowledge of the subject area or because they possess relevant skills. The role of the project team will be to play a full and equitable role in the five stages of project management.

Other groups

The project team may wish to establish other groups to help with particular aspects of the project – for example, to assist with diagnosis and understanding customer needs or to assist with aspects of implementation.

A project communications plan

A project communications plan is a critical element for securing successful projects. Its purpose is to ensure there are no surprises – so that everyone likely to be effected by the proposed change is informed at each milestone and involved/consulted appropriately.

This will minimise the likelihood of confusion and resistance.

Stage two: Problem analysis and diagnosis

The purpose of the second stage is to develop a shared and educated understanding of the nature of the problem and how things work at present. Project management helps us to:

- Find the root causes of problems and consider causes that may have been hidden from us. **(Step 2)**
- Prioritise further consideration of those aspects of a problem that, if tackled, will lead to the greatest leverage to make a qualitative difference. **(Step 3)**

Stage three: Developing options for change

The purpose of this third stage is to ensure that any change is prompted by a vision. Project management should not just be about solving problems, but it should capitalise on the opportunity to provide the optimum service or product. Likely tasks within this stage would be:

- Developing a vision of what the ideal service or product might look like. **(Step 4)**
- Understanding explicitly customer (*) needs.
- Considering scenarios in terms of maximising efficiency, meeting customer needs, managing staff concerns and considering organisational practicality.
- Setting short-term, medium-term and long-term goals that can assist the realistic progression towards a vision. **(Step 5)**
- Using customer* feedback to test the viability of the vision.
- Gaining commitment to the vision from those affected by it. **(Step 6)**

(*A customer is anyone on the receiving end of a service. Customers can be internal, such as HR providing recruitment support, or external.)

147

Stage Four: Devise an implementation plan

The purpose of this fourth stage is to agree a plan for realising the vision and effecting change. Likely tasks within this stage would be:

- Thinking creatively to discover all the possible options and resources for delivering the agreed vision. **(Step 7)**
- Agreeing on the best fit. **(Step 8)**
- Agreeing the establishment of a measuring and monitoring system. **(Step 9)**
- Developing a critical path or change management plan for action and implementation. **(Step 9)**
- Ensuring resources and their efficient use.
- Briefing and reassuring staff.
- Analysing and managing resistance.
- Meeting staff training needs.

Stage Five: Implementation, measurement and review

The purpose of this fifth and final stage is to address issues of implementation, measurement and review. Implementation should come relatively easy if the previous stages have been tackled properly. Measurement should not simply be a bureaucratic exercise but more a tool by which success can be demonstrated and learning opportunities highlighted. Likely tasks within this stage would be:

- Monitoring implementation. **(Step 9** onwards)
- Measuring outcomes – qualitatively and quantitatively.
- Reviewing and then making adjustments.
- Communicating learning, success, progress and enthusiasm.
- Proving support to staff and others affected by change.
- Consolidating gains.
- Standing down the project team. (An implementation team may be needed which may involve some members of the original project team, but will likely need other members with different skill sets and interests.)

> **33. Apply the Project Way Of Working (PWOW)**
> **approach to priority areas for improvement.**
> **Make the results and learning visible as soon as**
> **possible.**

Project way of working
(Example meeting by meeting)

1st meeting	Stage 1, Step 1

- Set the climate:
    - Make introductions; help reduce anxiety levels.
    - Set standards and ground rules.
- Clarify roles.
- Explain the approach.
- Introduce the project proposal. (Refer to example form within Project Way of Working, T&T No 22.)
- Use brainstorming to share perceptions of the current situation.
- Use the proposal form to guide discussion around the Project.
- Agree actions before next meeting (e.g. informal data gathering and communication).

2nd meeting	Stage 2, Steps 2 and 3

- Feedback on acceptance of proposal from the senior manager or sponsor.
- Further input of any new information is offered following informal data gathering.
- Agreement as to the approach to data gathering and action as to who's doing what between now and next meeting.
- Agree basic agenda for next meeting re presentation of data.

3rd meeting	Stage 2, Steps 2 and 3

- Present findings from data gathering.
- Agree   root causes
               priority issues   } as appropriate.
               leverage points
- Agree further actions to validate findings.

Stage 3, Step 4

- Brainstorm preferred outcome relevant to the above (Vision building).
- Agree to shape the brainstorm into a 'Vision' statement for next meeting.
- Agree communication/consultation actions.

4th meeting	**Stage 3, Step 4, 5 and 6**

- Present project 'Vision'
- Gain reaction, feedback and adjust accordingly.
- Agree major 'goals'.
- Test Commitment.

Stage 4, Step 7

- Brainstorm action to achieve goals.

Stage 4, Step 8

- Agree process for putting together an action plan.

5th meeting	*Stage 4, Step 9*

- Present proposal action plan (build up a critical path).
- Agree first steps.
- Present critical path to steering group.

6th meeting	*Stage 5*

- Agree implementation process. (May require a new team.)
- Implement.

7th meeting	

- Review success of first steps.
- Agree monitoring and reporting process.

Imagine everyone in the organisation having a common understanding and shared language about what managing change and improvement in the context of projects was all about. Immediately, you begin to create an increased awareness of the importance of 'prevention' and the following 'healthy' phrases begin to become everyday language:

- What stage is your project at?
- So, what are you trying to achieve – have you set your goals yet?
- What data gathering methods did you use to find out what is really going on?

- Who is your leader and sponsor?
- When do you expect to come up with an implementation plan?
- How has your communication plan changed from the start to now?
- What measures are you using to monitor progress?
- What tools and techniques have you found most useful?
- How much has your project proposal changed since you have found out the root cause of the problem?

If you ask yourself to what extent are these phrases in common use in your current organisation and the answer is 'hardly at all' then the next question should be: 'So what approach are you using to manage improvements and healing?'

The advantage of a common or shared approach is that it makes shared learning easier, taking the advantage of best practice across the whole of the organisation. It aids in monitoring progress and measuring results and has the potential for creating a database accessible to everyone who wants to be able at the touch of a button to find out what improvement initiatives are happening, where and at what stage they are at.

When our bodies heal we immediately become aware of improvement. The scar becomes less visible, the temperature reduces, our appetite returns, we have more energy, etc. Our monitoring and feedback mechanisms are internally connected to our overall 'system' of wellbeing.

Organisations need the same connections. A system whereby monitoring of improvement can be incorporated in a way that makes sense to the overall wellbeing of the organisation.

By adopting a project way of working, regular updates can be fed initially into the steering group and then, as projects grow, into a database.

It is important that the application of this approach emphasises creativity, actions, learning, working smarter and reduces inefficiency, bureaucracy, hierarchy and other analytical approaches to project management.

As indicated earlier, meetings are the most expensive way of communicating and decision-making. Therefore the meeting experience utilising the PWOW approach needs to epitomise the desired behaviours and values of the desired culture – in the case of 'Quality Through Leadership', a culture of learning, openness, creativity, action, initiative taking, respect and teamwork.

The values and behaviours are all healing, preventative behaviours and need to become 'the way we do things'. Another tangible opportunity whereby these can be encouraged and applied directly to improving people's work environment is through the process of 'Quality Action Teams'.

Quality Action Teams

The following are a few cases of Quality Action Team experiences:

A group of domestic assistants, working on the ward of a community psychiatric unit for the elderly, decided to review their work schedule with the help of a facilitator. After an observation that the routine of collecting the water jugs by the bed of each patient, and replacing them with fresh water three times a day, meant 90% of the time, they were pouring away full jugs of water to refill them again.

A question was raised – 'is this the best way to ensure patients get enough to drink?' When this information was passed on to the nursing staff, it transformed the way patients were encouraged to drink and the domestic staff saved both time and water! (See page 35.)

A team of 'order pickers' in an electrical distribution company formed a 'Quality Action Team' around the issue of inaccurately picked orders. They discovered that some of the labelling of similar components was unclear and confusing, some trays with small parts were overflowing and getting mixed with similar components, and the forms which the orders were picked from were sometimes unclear. Rather than check for clarification, the pickers, in their drive to achieve their targets (x amount of orders picked in x amount of time), second-guessed what was written on the form.

Once these contributing factors to the problem were identified, it became relatively easy to improve as the number of returned orders were reduced due to more accurate order-filling.

The following example is taken from *54 Tools and Techniques for Business Excellence,* Technique N° 52, page 234.

Seven secretaries who worked in a team to support the senior managers and academic staff of a college were invited to come together in a Quality Action Team format.

A facilitator helped to create an atmosphere between them where they could, without blame, identify many inefficient and frustrating work practices.

The main problems revolved around lack of team work, suspicions that work was not being divided up equally, favouritism by the management team, confusion over who was responsible for things like car park passes, stationery budget, room booking, even to what seems trivial but a major frustration – the cleaning of the kitchen and making coffee for visitors.

Other problems related to the way work was passed from the academic staff to the secretaries and how some staff insisted on only using certain individuals.

Unreasonable short term requests combined with poor response time to computer breakdown all contributed to a difficult working environment. The relief from the secretaries when all this became discussable was visible on their faces.

After several meetings and a presentation to the senior managers and some key academic staff, roles were clarified and improvements made.

The secretaries decided to meet at least once a fortnight for an hour to check progress, recognising that teamwork in a pool situation was essential for creating a healthy working environment.

It can be seen that no matter what business you are in – whether it's manufacturing, health, service or education – the potential for improving at an operational level is vast. Once you give permission and support the team with some structure, staff will be more than willing to improve their own work situation. If this is followed up with appropriate recognition then people taking personal responsibility for improvement begin to create a very healthy momentum of change.

The following is a step by step guide to managing a Quality Action Team:

Quality Action Teams – step by step guide

Imagine an organisation where staff working together took it upon themselves to use brainstorming (see 54 *Tools and Techniques for Business Excellence* Technique N° 40) and Pareto (54 *Tools and Techniques for Business Excellence* Technique N° 13) to identify things that they could do to improve their own work situation and/or methods.

Imagine all these staff having already experienced being part of a successful brainstorming exercise, and all understanding what 'the cost of failure' (54 *Tools and Techniques for Business Excellence* Technique N° 26) means. What if, as a result of this, they want to immediately apply this experience to improving their own local work situation?

What if some of these teams needed some help and support to get going, to set groundrules and plan ahead, and that this help was available from trained facilitators?

Imagine all managers and supervisors actually creating a work environment where this type of team activity is encouraged.

Quality Action Teams are small local work-related teams, acting on their own initiatives to improve working methods and practices that they have control and responsibility for, such as teams of administrative staff sharing facilities or working for the same supervisor.

They are characterised by short meetings, and high energy, and are action-orientated but still respect the key elements of effective problem-solving.

A typical schedule could look like this:

1. Recognition of the need to improve things – informal conversation and agreement to have a short meeting.

2. First meeting:
   - Set groundrules.
   - Clarify purpose.
   - Brainstorm failure activities (avoid solutions at this stage).
   - Prioritise (3 votes each).
   - There may be some obvious quick fixes as a result of good quality communication – if so, fine!
   - Commit to go back and gather more information about what's really going on regards priority failure activity.

   (This meeting may take between 30 – 60 minutes.)

3. Second Meeting:
   - Short check – how's it going?
   - What information have we got?
   - What new things have we learned regarding what's contributing to our failure costs/activities?
   - Brainstorm the ideal (the outcome we want either on one specific issue or the full work situation). What should it look like?
   - 'Hold the ideal' – think about, check it out.
   - Talk to other colleagues.

   (Meeting may take 30 to 45 minutes.)

4. Third Meeting:
   - Agree what the team want to achieve.
   - Brainstorm – how many ways can we think of to achieve this?
   - Choose the best ones.
   - Commit to taking first steps – tentatively at first – involving others who may not have been at the meeting.

   (Again – short meeting taking 30 to 45 minutes.)

5. Final Meeting:
   - How's it going?
   - What worked?
   - What hasn't worked?

- Can we improve things further?
- What sensibly can we do?
- Do we need to involve anyone else?
- Do we need help?
- Can we make visible what we have achieved so far and keep going?

(Meeting may take 30 minutes.)

The above description is just one way of managing a Quality Action Team process. Some teams manage to go through the improvement cycle without formal meetings but with a conscious effort during work time, in breaks to:

- Identify problems.
- Clarify ideal outcome.
- Implement things they can.

Others build the process into established meeting forums.

Essentially, it's giving people permission to take charge of their own improvement agenda and giving this support by providing:

- Supportive work environment.
- Tools and techniques.
- Facilitation, if needed.

So, it can be seen from this chapter that to get everyone involved in quality improvement in a way that sustains health and wealth, several organisational systems and structures need to be in place:

- A structure to cascade and communicate.
- A system for collating failure activities.
- A structure for facilitators to work together.
- A structure to manage projects of improvement.
- A system to monitor the progress of projects.
- A structure to encourage staff, at all levels, to implement improvements within their own sphere of control.

---

34. Offer the opportunity for everyone in the organisation to be involved in Quality Action Teams.

To achieve healing organisation status, this level of focused enthusiasm needs to be maintained. The challenge will be to embed the practices in the culture. This will require redesign of processes, reviews of policies and effective human resource management, in particular staff appraisal or personal performance management.

In the next chapter, we will discover the pitfalls and opportunities this presents, amusingly illustrated in the capable hands of Daphne, our Personnel Director of Delectrex Limited.

6

Nourishment

We are what we eat. We become what we think. Eating a balanced diet, engaging in healthy activity and continuously being open to learning new things are the prerequisites of a healthy life style. Nourishment in all its forms – food, exercise and ideas – are the fuels needed to energise ourselves in becoming what we want – or at least enjoying what we've got!

Within an organisational or work context, the issues are the same.

Information, communication, open forums, educational events, social events, work/life balance policies, healthy lifestyle promotion, visits to other organisations, wellbeing facilities at work, caring and supportive styles of supervision and effective reward and recognition policies are all examples of organisational nourishment.

Without these, the organisation will be malnourished, ill-informed, lacking in direction, with people feeling uncared for, not listened to and undervalued. This will eventually lead to emaciation (people leaving), de-motivation, a slowing of performance and an increase in sickness rates. Having a strategic policy of healthy organisational nourishment will significantly contribute to sustainability – a key component of the healing organisation.

So, how is this sustainable, nourishing policy working in practice?

Delectrex Limited

One of the most productive and creative partnerships developed over the last 18 months had been between Daphne, the Personnel Director (now HR Director) and the Quality Through Leadership programme manager Alison (now the Assistant Director of Organisation Development). Alison had made her mark. She had quickly gained the confidence and respect of the workforce (apart from Graham, stalwart of the staff representative group) with her bubbly, enthusiastic and down to earth style. She has an amazing ability to link the theory of 'healing organisation' with operational life.

Alison worked directly for Daphne, and Daphne had gained greatly from Alison's experience and had transformed the way 'personnel' operated and was perceived.

Daphne's department was small, but significant. It consisted of two personnel officers, one training manager and two administrative assistants. With Alison's help, it had gone from a Personnel policy and control department which was continually inundated with problems related to recruitment, absence, sickness, discipline, etc., to a department perceived as a Human Resource support unit offering consultancy to managers who were now taking more responsibility on all matters personnel.

The atmosphere was getting tense in Daphne's office which closely resembled a greenhouse/alternative therapy shop!

"This is bloody ridiculous. Last year we only got an inflation-related pay rise and now you're asking some of the women who are among the lowest-paid to pay £20 a month subsidy for the crèche facility!" 'Grey' Graham was a foreboding figure – tall, bearded with his 30 years experience telling a little by his continuous frustration over the many changes implemented in the last year.

Daphne tried to reason with him: "But Graham, we didn't have a crèche a few months ago and only implemented as it was a major issue amongst our younger part-time mums – it's costing us to run it and the subsidy helps, and surely it saves them on childcare costs?"

"It's just another way of getting them to comply with the new shift system," retorted Graham suspiciously.

"Oh, come off it, Graham. The staff have never had it so good!" Alison couldn't contain herself any longer.

"What do you know? You haven't even been here five minutes!" Graham raised his voice.

"OK, that's enough you two. It's about time you two buried the hatchet," Daphne injected.

Yeah, right into his thick skin, Alison wished. "OK, so what *do* you want, Graham?"

The meeting dragged on, ending in an agreement to go back to the crèche users to ask what a reasonable subsidy should be.

Alison, still fuming, turned to Daphne. "Why is he still here? He's caused so many problems and has hidden behind his union status for years. He is not good at his job and . . ."

"Woah, Alison. This is not like you. He's really got to you, hasn't he?" Daphne tried to calm her down.

"I just don't like bullies and if his boss had conducted performance appraisals a few years ago – as we are now – he would either be a changed man, or out!"

"You're an idealist Alison. There are always going to be die-hards like Graham. We have done well to get him involved in the partnership initiative with all our unions. We need to keep him on side. I have an idea up my sleeve, but let's get off him and get on to the big agenda item, how to present and communicate the results of the staff survey!"

*　*　*　*　*

The boardroom was crowded. Dave had increased the regular executive team meeting to include all of the Department Heads. The air was mixed with anticipation, curiosity, excitement and the smell of freshly brewed coffee.

"OK, Alison – over to you." Dave sat poised with pen in hand. Although he knew what was coming, he was curious as to how his team would react.

"Thanks Dave. There's good and bad news. The good news is that we got a 70% return for the staff survey which is above average for a return – and the bad news is, the results are not as good as we expected especially in two of our priority improvement areas: communication and IT. So here goes . . . ."

*　*　*　*　*

"So, this is where you rule from?" Ged looked around at the wood-panelled walls, the inspirational posters, the mahogany desk and captains' chair, the oval board table and the impressive coffee machine bubbling away in the corner. He smiled at the one and only golf trophy in the display cabinet.

"Good to see you, Ged. Thanks for coming. It makes a change from the golf course!" Dave had persuaded a reluctant Ged to make a visit after agreeing to review the survey results.

"Did you get a chance to look around, Ged?"

"Yes, Dan proudly showed me the warehouse and shop, and Daphne took me through the sales office and gave me an update on what you have been doing on the HR front – very impressive!" Ged had been out of consultancy for a while now, but recognised an inventive and modern practice.

"Exactly!" Dave said. "So, why are the staff survey results so bad?"

"They're not," Ged calmly replied.

Dave looked confused, leant forward and said "Go on then, Ged – explain – make my day!"

"Right, listen – here's a list of what you have done over the last year:

- Revised the appraisal process and trained managers in coaching skills.
- Empowered a group of trained facilitators to encourage staff to work on problems and failure activities.
- Introduced personal development planning and career counselling.

- Introduced e-learning and encouraged access for all by providing computer access learning points in the warehouse and offices.
- Introduced a flexible working hours option.
- The regular team briefing is well attended.

. . . and now you're talking about discount options at the local gym and the promise of end of year bonus depending on company results."

"So, they should be bloody grateful – yes?!" Dave shifts out of his chair and leans over to Ged. "Tell me honestly, Ged – no bullshit – what's going on? How can 50% of the workforce say communication is still poor and IT support is still inadequate?"

"It's to be expected, Dave. You have raised the bar! They now know what's possible and their expectations have increased. They are more prepared to be honest about what's really going on. You have to ask yourself:

- Has morale improved?
- Has production increased?
- Are the number of complaints and returns down?
- Is customer satisfaction up?
- Are profits up?"

"Well, yes to all of those questions actually, Ged!" Dave smugly replies.

"Then what's the problem?" Ged excitedly asks.

"You mean – I don't have one?"

"Well, actually you do – it relates to how you communicate these results to the rest of the staff, in a way that motivates them to keep improving and shows them that you are listening, by doing something to improve yourself!"

"Improve myself? I think I've done quite a bit of that in the last year – what else do I have to do?" Dave began to wilt a little – exasperated and uncertain as to what his friendly consultant was getting at.

"A lot of the staff survey results are to do with perception. Look at these questions:

- Do our managers know what's going on?
- Do the senior team care about what we do?
- Are the senior team are visible?
- Is the senior team is accessible?

Only 45% replied positively to these questions – do you think that's a fair result?"

"I suppose so, but what more can I do?"

Dave and Ged talked a little further and explored the options of walking the shopfloor more often, regularly posting notices about improvements and being more robust in publishing progress reports about improvement projects.

160

"You see, Dave, people forget how bad it used to be. People start taking the new ways of working for granted. It's still early days. To achieve a self-sustaining healing culture, people need to be involved in the process of improvement and need constant reminding about the connection between values, behaviours and what you are trying to achieve with Quality Through Leadership. You need to do this until you have a critical mass of champions to keep the momentum going. By the way, I met Alison. All you need is half a dozen more Alisons and you can sit back and concentrate on your golf swing."

"Ha, now you're talking, Ged – see you on the course on Saturday?"

"You bet!"

It can be seen from what's going on at Delectrex Limited that this now is a very different company from 18 months ago. A massive investment in people has created a working environment where there is a greater level of ownership and care about what is going on at every level. Expectations are raised and there is a thirst for more. Dave Battle's challenge now is to harness this energy and keep the momentum going.

The healing organisation diet can be summarised in the following ways:

- Staff appraisal/Performance management.
- Training and development.
- Welfare.
- Reward and recognition.

Staff appraisal/Performance management

Take a look at the following list of behaviours. They are all positive and have been described by staff as behaviours they value from their boss.

I value a boss who:

1. Gets full commitment from staff; knows their capabilities; encourages; considers their feelings and aspirations.
2. Has strength of purpose; is willing to deal with important issues head on, no matter how tough.
3. Does his job for the company and the customer; gives 110% effort; sees self as part of the team.
4. Is open and honest; approachable and dependable; a good listener. Displays interest in other people's points of view.

5. Will take action. Has a 'let's go for it' attitude.
6. Will discuss decisions and listens to arguments. Disseminates all relevant information.
7. Inspires confidence; is trustworthy. Communicates clearly how decisions are made.
8. Delegates. Demonstrates trust and encourages ownership of problems.
9. Asks for people's ideas. Is prepared to be persuaded by logical, relevant discussion.
10. Cares about people and their problems. Is interested on a personal level.
11. Sets realistic objectives with clear criteria and groundrules.
12. Knows what is going on. Has a big picture. Looks at problems globally. Can communicate the company view.

These behaviours were elicited from staff as part of a research project in a large telecommunications company. The staff were also asked to rank them in order of importance, and the overall result is as set out above.

The research was conducted in one company, and it was some years ago, but my experience since that date leads me to believe that it is as valid today as it was when I first undertook it, if not more so.

I have used the same list of behaviours to ask staff in other companies which 'boss behaviour' they most experience and which is the one they least experience? From an international airline, to the National Health Service, the feedback is consistent – most of the time, number one is experienced least and it's often the harder edge behaviour, number 5, that is experienced most.

---

35. Listen to the aspirations of your staff, understand their feelings and hopes for a better work experience.

Staff want a boss to listen to them, to value their contribution and to support them in their hopes and aspirations. People respect and respond well to an empathic boss, who is skilled at understanding the special contribution any worker can offer, given a chance.

Yet this behaviour is so valued by staff but is rarely experienced. At best, it may be visible during an annual appraisal, at worst – the appraisal may not happen or it becomes a 'tick in the box' exercise.

Managers often make the mistake of perceiving the appraisal of staff as a job to fit in once a year around everything else, rather than what it should be – a core element of the manager's role and an opportunity to improve performance through the coaching and development of their staff.

Part of the problem is that managers are usually promoted because they were effective at their previous job, not because of any skill in appraising their staff. Managers are not always skilled at appraisal or coaching and therefore find it difficult and uncomfortable. As humans, we tend to spend time on the things we enjoy and avoid the things we find difficult. This all contributes to managers avoiding planning in appraisal time as a priority.

Some of the reasons for avoidance relate to the procedure itself. If it is complex and bureaucratic, with many forms, many standards, and multiple signatures, this can be a disincentive. Better to keep it simple and developmental, conducted in a coaching style.

> **36. Make performance management/appraisal a priority – do not leave it as a 'last minute' or 'once a year' task to be fitted in.**

I have seen many appraisal schemes and the better ones follow the principles below:

- Standards and competencies related to the job in question are clear.
- Appraisals are conducted twice a year.
- The appraiser follows a coaching framework linked to the problem-solving/improvement process, i.e.

PRESENT	How do you think you have done so far? To what extent have you achieved your goals? What are your strengths? (What are you good at?) What do you find most difficult?
FUTURE	What can we agree that should be in place within the next 6 months/1 year? Ideally, what creative and challenging vision do you want for yourself? Tell me about your ambitions. Let's agree the targets and goals for the next 6 months.

ACTION	What's your first thoughts about achieving these goals? What sort of things are you going to have to do? What are the first steps? What support have you got? What help do you need from me?

Answers to these questions will give the opportunity for the manager to listen, demonstrate understanding and offer his/her own personal feedback so an agreed and shared perception of performance can be achieved.

- The appraised gets a chance to write their own reflections and insights and these are carried over to a personal development plan that the appraised keeps and updates on a regular basis.
- Answers to the support questions in the 'Action' stage should elicit any Training and Development needs which should be processed into a central company Training Needs Analysis, and followed up by both parties.

> **37. Engender a climate of self responsibility for personal development with access to a rich variety of resources for learning.**

Occasionally, you will come across a situation when, despite best efforts, a staff member repeatedly fails to come up to the mark. It is important to have clear and well defined disciplinary procedures and it helps if managers are trained in challenging skills (page 202).

No one should ever be surprised when disciplined. Appropriate support and feedback should have been given before this 'failure' activity reluctantly happens.

On the other hand, staff should also be clear about the rewards which are possible. Any scheme needs to be transparent and fair. Whether it is an end-of-year bonus, a percentage increase in pay, additional holidays, educational visits or promotion to the next level on the pay scale – they all need to be linked to the appraisal process and given on merit.

> **38. Reward those behaviours consistent with supporting the development of the healing organisation.**

The appraisal process is a good opportunity to reinforce the values and behaviours of the 'healing organisation'. Adding the following questions to the appraisal can reinforce individuals' responsibility to organisation wide improvement:

- To what extent has the staff member improved their own work situation?
- To what extent has the staff member worked in a team to solve problems and contribute to a better way of working?
- To what extent has the staff member contributed to team briefings (attendance/questions)?
- To what extent has the staff member contributed to Quality Through Leadership workshops and training?
- To what extent has the staff member contributed to the Project Way of Working?
- To what extent has the staff member contributed to Staff Survey (acted on results)?
- To what extent has the staff member contributed to teamwork?
- To what extent has the staff member contributed to improved communication?
- To what extent has the staff member contributed to leadership development?

The behaviours described above can be tailored, depending on the level of work, but the principle of 'as a manager you get what you reward' is a powerful one and the appraisal process is a great opportunity to feed the staff with guidance about what makes a healthy thriving work environment. Sharing your vision and reinforcing company or team values at this time can be motivational and supportive.

Some organisations have limited opportunities for career development and financial incentives. This should not be a reason for paying lip service to the appraisal process.

A good appraisal can be a reward in itself. If you combine this with being creative and flexible in how jobs are changed and designed to take advantage of people's skills, then even in absence of financial reward and direct promotion, you will, through a coaching and developmental appraisal process, motivate and reward staff.

The need for recognition, to be valued and to belong are basic human needs. These basic needs can partly be realised at that time of year when an honest and healthy dialogue takes place between staff and boss. Ideally, it becomes a learning partnership where the boss also demonstrates a willingness to learn from feedback given by staff as to how well they feel they have been managed.

The following questionnaire (linked to the same research mentioned previously) has been used by managers to distribute to their team in a quest for honest feedback. In doing so, they create the opportunity to reinforce effective leadership behaviours and model the behaviour they expect their teams to show. The questionnaire is a list of the skills needed to demonstrate the leadership behaviours listed on page 161.

Leadership skills questionnaire

This questionnaire is designed to help you assess your strengths and weaknesses on a number of leadership skills.

On the following pages, you will be given a number of leadership behaviours. You will be asked to rate yourself on these skills, on a scale of 1 to 5. A score of '1' indicates your lowest rating; a score of '5' indicates your highest rating. You should rate yourself by circling the appropriate number on this scale. For example, in rating your response to behaviour (A) "Listening to others effectively", if you feel that you are very good at listening to others you should circle 5.

By completing this self-assessment, you should be able to identify your own strengths and weaknesses. This will allow you to focus on areas which may need attention back in the workplace.

All the information collected will be for your own benefit, so complete it as accurately as possible.

Once you have completed your self-assessment, complete another assessment, this time based on your knowledge, observation and perception of your colleague. Again, the more honest the assessment, the more valuable it is. Your colleague will be doing the same for you.

When you have both completed the questionnaires, compare results and discuss the differences in how you see yourself and how your colleague sees you.

Quality Leadership Skills – Evaluation
(© Michael Wash, University of Leeds)

Please consider the following list and rate YOURSELF and your COLLEAGUE on each skill, by circling the appropriate number on the scale 1-5.

		LOW				HIGH
A)	Listening to others effectively.	1	2	3	4	5
B)	Reflecting back what others have said to check understanding.	1	2	3	4	5
C)	Asking open questions.	1	2	3	4	5
D)	Challenging what people have said in a constructive, non-threatening way.	1	2	3	4	5
E)	Giving appropriate, on-going feedback to others.	1	2	3	4	5
F)	Acknowledging and praising what others do and say.	1	2	3	4	5
G)	Recognising and valuing the strengths and potential in others.	1	2	3	4	5
H)	Recognising and valuing your own strengths and potential.	1	2	3	4	5
I)	Always being open to learning from staff.	1	2	3	4	5
J)	Having a clear process for making decisions, which is logical and effective.	1	2	3	4	5
K)	Communicating your plans and objectives clearly.	1	2	3	4	5
L)	Communicating up-to-date and relevant information to others.	1	2	3	4	5
M)	Communicating your own direction and vision to others.	1	2	3	4	5
N)	Being clear about your own job and responsibilities.	1	2	3	4	5

O)	Taking ownership and responsibility for your own job.	1	2	3	4	5
P)	Demonstrating commitment to issues by taking action.	1	2	3	4	5
Q)	Working well within a team.	1	2	3	4	5
R)	Making myself available to others and giving them enough of my time.	1	2	3	4	5
S)	Delegating work appropriately.	1	2	3	4	5

Scores

This commentary is of interest only. The real value in the exercise is the dialogue between self and colleague helping each other understand the ratings in context of the work they do.

80 – 95   I suspect you have a slightly inflated opinion of your own ability – check it out!

70 – 80   You are an excellent communicator and personal organiser of priorities. You delegate well, and work effectively within the team. People recognise you as supportive, and can always rely on you for feedback. An effective leader.

50 – 70   A competent communicator and team worker most of the time. You are likely to have your good and bad days. Generally, scoring well in most areas, I suspect you have a number of weaknesses and these, no doubt, will affect other categories. By identifying the circumstances in which these weaknesses become apparent, it will be possible to design a development plan to strengthen them.

38 – 50   You lack confidence in many areas. Seek out objective data and build on your strengths. Identify the areas you feel are the most important and ask for assistance to design opportunities to improve these.

19 – 38   You probably survive by not working with people! You are isolated, or the job does not warrant people skills. Either that or you need help in boosting your self-image!

The results, discussed openly in a group will promote interesting debate about clarity of decision-making, delegation, communication and other essential ingredients for effective leadership.

This is the food of management! These processes enrich relationships, nourish the experience of work and become part of the armoury of medicine contributing to organisational health!

Training and development

The term 'training and development' combines two essential aids to human advancement, but it is surprising how many people do not understand the difference between the two.

A healing organisation will have an Education, Training and Development strategy.

The table below will help distinguish the differences:

Education	Training	Development
• Increasing knowledge • Presentation of the facts • Researching information • Reading updates • Briefing News	• Job focused • Short/medium term • Specific • Skill based • Instruction • Workshop/event based or • On the job training • Computer based • Qualification or Competency • Recognition • Enhance job performance	• Person focused • Long term • General • Attitude/Personality/Style • Mentoring • All situations are an opportunity • Personal improvement • Practice and review of experience • Confidence in self • Life changes/choices

To help distinguish between these in an obvious way, you only have to ask the question to a group of parents with young children: 'How many of you would be happy if your child came home and said "Mum/Dad, today we had sex education"?' There would be no objection in the audience. However, if you asked them how they would feel if their child came home and said 'Mum/Dad, today we had sex training', then you would get a very different response! Sex development of course then comes into a longer-term issue of body/biological development and increased awareness and choices related to sexuality.

It is important to understand that appropriate methods of increasing the workforce competency can be designed, based on actual organisation and personal need.

Central to the 'healing' theme is sustainability. Sustainability can be achieved at every level in the organisation if 'self responsibility' for personal development is encouraged, within a climate of learning opportunity.

This learning opportunity climate needs to be one where there is clarity about the expected level of competency required to be successful. What does each job demand in terms of knowledge (education), skill level (training) and application (development)?

Each job needs to be evaluated in terms of what the organisation needs, both in respect of present demands and future challenges. (This latter point is particularly important when recruiting.)

A definition of learning I use is 'new insight that brings about the option for an increased range of personal choices'. In the context of organisational healing, we are encouraging 'personal empowerment'. This empowerment relates to individuals in any job situation having the confidence and freedom to initiate improvement related to the objective of that job. Whether it is answering the phone, collecting refuse, delivering post, teaching or managing a production process – the person on the job needs to feel that they have 'job control' and personal responsibility, are valued, and have the ability, with support, to initiate local change and improvements. This is a symbiotic relationship between individual and boss, department and organisation, where alignment of purpose and recognition of good practice is regularly highlighted in the way people work together. This can be done through regular team or department review meetings, where people are encouraged to highlight successes and frustrations with the aim of identifying opportunities for improvement.

Essentially, we are describing here the need to move from a dependant workforce to an empowered workforce. This transition can be illustrated in the following taxonomy of development modes, originally described in research from Sheffield Polytechnic and a consultancy firm 'Transform Limited'.

Development modes
(Adapted from Boydell & Leary (1996)[9] and Pedlar, Burgoyne & Boydell (1997)[10].

1. **Avoiding** – 'sticking to the rules'
   - My job is my job. Anything beyond that is not my responsibility. I do not take initiative other than that directed to me by my job description and my boss.

---

[9] Boydell, T. & Leary, M., *Identifying Training Needs*, CIPD, 1996
[10] Pedlar, M., Burgoyne, J. & Boydell, T., *The Learning Company – A Strategy for Sustainable Development*, 2nd ed, McGraw-Hill, 1997

- A key characteristic of this aspect of development from an employee perspective is **Dependency**.

2. **Controlling** – 'running a tight ship'
   - I must know what is going on, no surprises – and ensure everything and everyone conforms to what I am confident about. I must make sure I cannot be blamed for things going wrong.
   - A key characteristic from an employer's perspective is **Creating Dependency**.

3. **Relating** – 'polishing performance'
   - I want to do well and I feel valued if I get feedback from others that I am doing what I am expected to do really well.
   - A key characteristic from an employee perspective is **Seek approval and recognition.**

4. **Experiencing** – 'not accepting what doesn't feel right'
   - While I know what is expected of me and I like getting recognition/ approval, I will stand up for what I don't think or feel is right. I have discovered that I want to be me and not just conform.
   - A key characteristic of this aspect of development from an employee perspective is **Owning my work**.

5. **Experimenting** – 'undertaking deliberate risk'
   - I realise things can get better and am willing to discover things for myself. I am prepared to move into new situations without the support of structure and rules.
   - A key characteristic of this aspect of development from anyone at work in this mode is **Managing Change**.

6. **Connecting** – 'being part of the bigger picture'
   - I develop with the confidence that my personal vision is congruent with the organisational vision.
   - **Valuing and respecting interdependency** – these individuals work towards a team, win-win approach at work.

7. **Integrating** – 'making work a part of my life'
   - My personal life's purpose is clear and aided by my current role. This is life enhancing creating a balance between the things that are important to me.
   - These individuals are **Purposeful** and congruent at work and home. All areas fulfilled and mutually supportive.

Developing a healing organisation requires a development strategy that encourages individuals to more toward the attainment of mode 6 and 7.

Mode 4 is the pivotal threshold when individuals begin to question what they are doing in the context of 'is there a better way?' In the context of improving efficiency and quality of service this is to be encouraged. However, it is fair to say that there are job situations where modes 1, 2 and 3 are preferred, such as military situations, conducting a surgical procedure or flying a plane!

To capitalise on individuals questioning the 'way we work' a climate of 'supportive risk taking' needs to develop – by which I mean risk in terms of experimenting with new ways of working, *not* risks to self, others or compromising health, safety or quality.

This move towards 'supportive risk taking' requires praise and reward moving away from recognising approval-seeking and conforming towards rewarding creativity, innovation and experimenting. Here, the benefits of the healing process begin to become tangible through the attainment of ever-increasing performance levels.

This climate of 'experimenting' can be encouraged by raising awareness of how individuals learn new levels of competence (see Figure 14).

In 'world class' organisations, you will find a critical mass of managers who know how to encourage learning through encouragement, coaching and a supportive style of delegation – knowing that they will need 'conscious competence' to continuously be in place if they are going to have a continual flow of talent ready and eager to take on additional responsibilities.

This learning climate, however, needs to be a partnership – this partnership being an important element of the symbiotic aligned relationship between organisation, department, boss and the individual.

For training and development to be focused and efficient, it needs to be based on need. An appropriate needs analysis should take place in the context of what all parties in this relationship are seeking to achieve. A focused discussion related to mutual expectations can be achieved through the appraisal process (page 161).

Each individual needs to own and progress their own personal development in the context of their personal ambition. (Refer to Personal Development Planning in *54 Tools and Techniques for Business Excellence,* Technique N° 49, page 213.)

---

39. Develop a learning partnership between boss and staff where both parties understand the implications of empowerment.

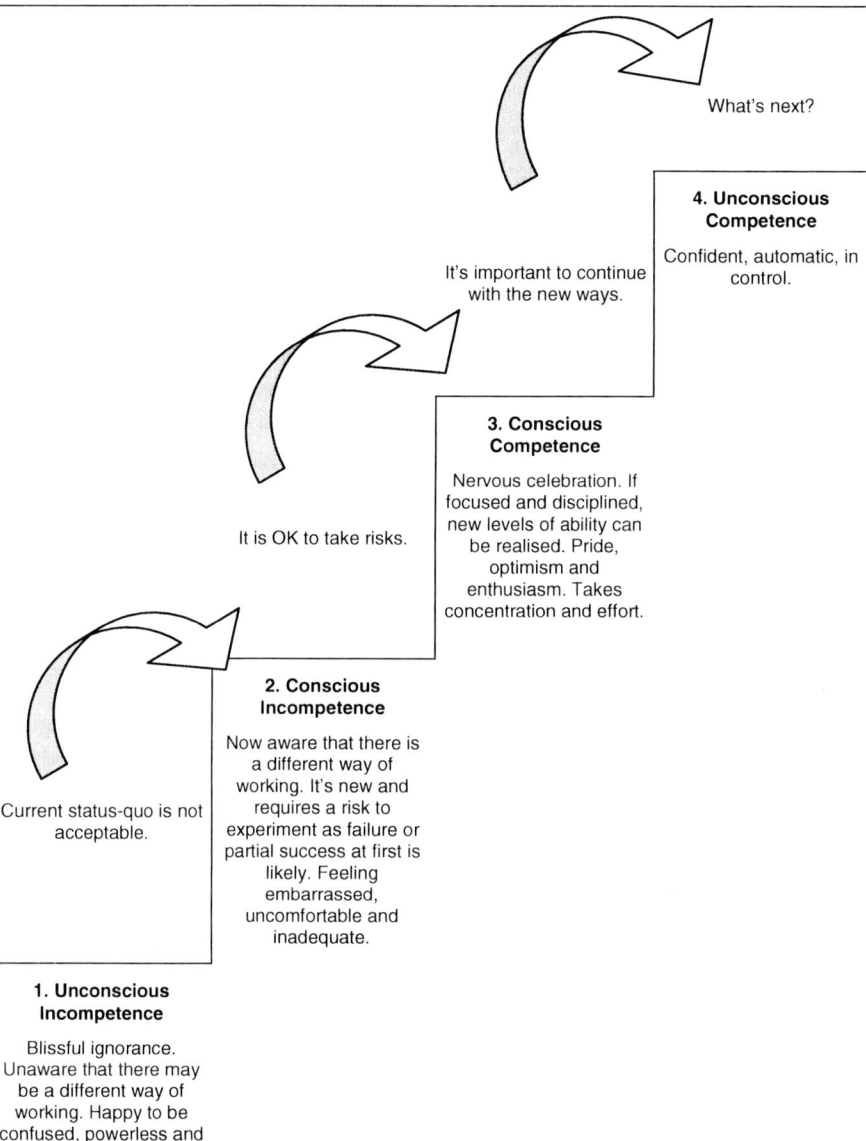

What's next?

4. Unconscious Competence

Confident, automatic, in control.

It's important to continue with the new ways.

3. Conscious Competence

Nervous celebration. If focused and disciplined, new levels of ability can be realised. Pride, optimism and enthusiasm. Takes concentration and effort.

It is OK to take risks.

2. Conscious Incompetence

Now aware that there is a different way of working. It's new and requires a risk to experiment as failure or partial success at first is likely. Feeling embarrassed, uncomfortable and inadequate.

Current status-quo is not acceptable.

1. Unconscious Incompetence

Blissful ignorance. Unaware that there may be a different way of working. Happy to be confused, powerless and dependent.

Figure 14. The steps of competence

The following table highlights key questions that can be used as part of a training needs analysis.

Individual	Organisation
• What do I want to achieve in my current role? • What support do I need? • What skills do I need to develop in order to increase my effectiveness? • What additional experience will improve my ability? • Where can I get the appropriate knowledge and information to support what I need to achieve? • What do I need to be more familiar with to improve my confidence and competence? • What do I need to develop to achieve my ambition?	• Do we have the right skill mix and competencies to achieve our Vision? • How is our people development strategy enhancing our succession planning? • What are the qualities, attitudes and behaviours needed for us to realise our ambitions? • How does the current level of skill and competency match our desired level of performance – where's the gap?

The matching between individual and organisational needs in the context of personal and organisational vision is important. If alignment of direction and values can be achieved then it's possible for everyone in the organisation to feel a contributory part of the healing process.

Line managers play a key role through coaching, appropriate delegation, and rewarding and recognising learning and improvement. This can be particularly effective when applied to specific training events. So often, individuals go on training events and their manager is oblivious to where they are and what they are doing. The manager needs to be part of the learning contract. 80% of new information, or new-found levels of 'conscious competence' is lost 72 hours after any training event, unless some reinforcement of the new learning takes place. The manager can be a crucial aid in this process.

---

40. Design a training and development strategy based on a formula that matches personal with organisational need.

When I conduct training or run workshops, or even conferences, I ensure the following process and questions are addressed:

Before the Event	After the Event
• What does the organisation/manager want to achieve? • What changes would they like to see in their staff? • How do they see themselves supporting the process? • The manager then needs to ask the staff who are to be trained: • What understanding do you have as to why you are going on this training? • What do you want to achieve? • What help do you need from me?	• How did you get on? • What was useful? • What new ideas and thoughts have you got about putting the learning into practice? • How can I help?

So, it can be seen from the above that the manager has a major stake in the successful development of his/her staff and this is conveyed through an active dialogue focused on the ambition of the individual and the organisation.

> **41. Every training episode should have a sponsor, i.e. someone who cares enough to explore with the trainee before and after the event, ways of getting the most out of the experience.**

Welfare

There are around 150,000 people injured and over 200 people killed doing their job each year in the UK. The health, safety and welfare of staff is a legal and critical responsibility of the employer and, ideally, a shared responsibility with the employee.

There is a direct correlation between how well staff are treated and cared for, and how well staff care for each other and the customer.

A brief summary and overview of staff welfare can be illustrated using the 'Welfare Wheel', see Figure 15.

> **42. Developing a positive welfare environment, while maintaining the customer focus, is the optimum formulae for successful staff in a successful business.**

Figure 15. The staff welfare wheel

Reward and recognition

Near the end of the job interview, the young, confident applicant was asked "What salary are you looking for?"

"Something in the region of £90,000, depending on the benefits package."

"Well, what would you say to a package of 6 weeks holiday, plus 12 paid holidays, full medical and dental cover and a new company car every year?"

"Wow, are you kidding?"

"Certainly. But you started it!".

Not everyone is motivated by the same things, but everyone wants a fair wage for a fair days' work. Beyond paying a competitive salary, what else motivates staff?

Many of the previously explored welfare elements are important for improving morale and motivation – e.g. job security, job satisfaction, working conditions, etc. So, how is the 'feel good' factor maintained at work? What else can be done to provide incentive, recognise and reward behaviour and performance? Firstly, let's distinguish between these three 'motivators':

Incentives	Recognition	Reward
• Clear targets linked to clear rewards. • Often used in Sales, e.g. commission or prizes for selling the most.	• Thanks, praise and/or acknowledgement of behaviour or performance in a tangible way. • Open, personal or by letter. • Can be made visible to all, e.g. photo of 'Employee of the Month'.	• Tangible, e.g. cash, extra holiday, voucher, educational visit, car parking space reserved, free lunch, bonus, share schemes, etc.

In some organisations I have worked in, there seems to be a resistance to praise. This is particularly evident in hard-edged male-dominated organisations, such as engineering and also vocational based service institutions such as the Health Service. A dominant theme from both types of organisation is: 'Why reward what they should be doing any way? That's what they get paid for.' This, of course, misses the point of incentive, recognition and reward – to create the opportunity to shape behaviour and performance to the type and level consistent with the company vision, values and culture.

It is important to be clear about the criteria used to recognise and reward staff. Transparent and open processes to all staff need to be communicated clearly and creatively so to avoid any scheme becoming institutionalised and hence de-motivating.

Any scheme needs to be fresh and exciting. Several of my clients design an annual award ceremony to recognise individuals and teams who have demonstrated not only extraordinary performance, but who have done it in a way that demonstrates learning, behaviour and techniques consistent with the desired values of the organisation. So things like teamwork, innovation, partnership and customer focus are all explicit criteria by which the contenders for the award need to excel in. These are great celebratory events.

Managers underestimate the power of public recognition. I was running a conference in a large hospital a few years ago and at the end, while summing up, I gave acknowledgement and thanks to my team member who worked hard, in the background, setting the event up.

> **43. Recognise, praise and reward the behaviours**
> **you want. Always say thank you.**

While I thanked him, I asked him to stand up – I walked up to him and shook his hand and said "Thank you". A round of applause followed. This was at the risk of embarrassing the poor chap, and of course it did – but that one symbolic gesture was talked about for months in relation to 'what is recognition?', 'why don't we praise more?' and 'what is it about our culture that creates discomfort when giving positive praise and feedback?' These are good questions all organisations should ask of themselves.

> **44. Celebrate success in a big way giving equal**
> **weight to results and learning.**

If you feel you are limited as to what rewards are available and what you can afford to give, then don't start by saying 'yes, but . . . .' or 'we can't because . . . .'

Start with what is ideally possible. Be creative. Brainstorm at least 54 ways of rewarding your staff. Here are a few ideas:

- Letters of thanks from managers to staff.
- Letters and points of praise posted on bulletin boards or the intranet or emailed.
- Quality prizes for contributions beyond what's expected.
- Reserved car parking space for 'employee of the month'.
- Team of the month/year.

- Extra time off, from a few hours, to a few days.
- Success story published in company newsletter.
- Travel award.
- Training voucher or Book or gift voucher.
- Membership fees/discount to local gym.
- Reward pins to be worn with pride.
- Share schemes.
- Bonus.
- Commission.
- Lunch.
- Cakes for the team.
- Discount on company products.
- Boss for the Day.
- Invitation to sit in to the Board or executive team meetings.
- The yellow jersey/tie/t-shirt.
- Trophy.
- Certificates.
- Long service awards.
- Retirement gifts, and many, many more. . . . . .

Any one, or a combination, of the above – however trivial it may seem – will make an impression. When you are on the receiving end of genuine recognition, it is always a big deal. It is about being valued and being seen to be contributing to the bigger picture. Believe me, it can make a significant difference to an individual who, perhaps for years, has been working hard, quietly without any acknowledgement, then all of a sudden realises he is important after all!

Developing a praise, recognition and reward culture will aid motivation and loyalty, but the challenge is to make it 'stick'. Make it a part of the way things are done, built on a genuine attitude of positive leadership.

This creates an air of confidence and increases the 'feel good' factor, even in the most challenging times.

As is the case when our health is at risk – the more positive the attitude, the greater the belief in the power of self healing and the greater the chance of survival and a healthy outcome, i.e. a cure.

> **45. Each manager needs to understand the power of positive thinking, having an optimistic outlook and understanding the value of highlighting the strengths in others.**

7

Cure

'Silence like a cancer grows' – the Simon and Garfunkel lyrics remind us all too well of the threats to our wellbeing, be it in a physical sense (cancer) or in a mental sense (silence).

Listening to ourselves and being in the company of others, where high quality communication is present, is probably the surest way of keeping in touch with reality.

When an organisation's ability to listen to itself and others is compromised, issues and conversations begin to live in the shadows. Negative issues begin to be become the norm. The corporate equivalent of toxic substances, carcinogens and abnormal growths are allowed to flourish – by not managing poor performance, not dealing with sexual harassment or bullying, ignoring the prejudice and lack of respect for diversity, poor standards, compromising health and safety, mistreatment of customers or patients/clients, and so on

These issues need confronting and dealing with before they become systemic, with 'bad blood' creating secondaries and becoming terminal – i.e. the negative behaviours and management's acceptance of them become the norm, institutionalised and, before long, staff are blind to what's going on.

Healing this type of situation requires courage and powerful, responsible leadership (Chapters 1 and 2).

This, with a strong continuous communication process, reinforcing the vision and values (Chapter 5) will help make 'disease' and 'dysfunctional' elements more visible.

Courage is needed to deal with these, by ensuring progressive policies are implemented and discrepant behaviours are dealt with.

Conventional treatment to disease is sometimes not enough.

Going beyond training, downsizing, cost cutting, re-engineering and use of consultants, will require a self-belief that a cure through 'self help' is possible – with a significant investment in 'creative' approaches to healthy living within the workplace.

To what extent can Dave Battle and his team get to the roots of the culture, to challenge what is really going on and begin to establish and demonstrate that it's the 'healing' values that are going to sustain growth and not dysfunctional custom and practice.

Delectrex Limited

"The traffic is getting worse on this ring road! Ever since they built the new shopping centre. Sorry I'm late, Matthew." Daphne usually enjoyed her morning pick-up run. Most mornings, she picked up Babs, Mr Battle's secretary, Thomas, the Transport Manager and Matthew, the in-house Sales Manager. It was a great chance for gossip and finding out what was really going on.

"It's OK, Daphy, no probs." Matthew was always upbeat and positive – a demeanour which had earned him the reputation of being able to sell snow to the Eskimos.

"I've phoned Thomas to tell him we are on our way."

"So Babs, what a lovely morning! And how are you this bright sunny morning?"

"I'm fine, thanks, Matthew." Babs replied in her usual and polite motherly manner.

Daphne pulled in to a lay-by where a waiting Thomas was sheepishly putting out his cigarette.

"Thought you had given up, Tom," shouted Matthew.

"I will do one day – but this week has been a bit difficult."

Daphne set off and turned the radio off. They had a twenty minute journey.

"Really, Tom, why's that?" Daphne loved these conversations.

The combination of Babs, Matthew and Thomas meant that she heard almost all of the gossip which helped her keep in touch with the general working climate.

Thomas went on to describe how he had to sack one of the delivery drivers last week. After a long investigation, it was discovered he was short-changing customers, not by much – but over the months, probably years, this had lead to quite a bit of stolen stock.

Matthew chirped up "Yep! About time – now we are really cleaning the place up! Get rid of all the dead wood, I say."

"Easier said than done." Daphne had been scarred by many employment review tribunals.

"Even so – the next step has got to be the Warehouse shop!"

"What's going on in there, then?" Daphne knew really, but was interested to know how much the others knew.

Matthew replied sharply "Well, I think we all know there has been a custom and practice for family and friends discounts going on for years! I don't think we should discuss it too much as I believe that something is going to happen soon." Changing the subject, Matthew deflected the question: "So, Babs and Daphne – what's the rumour about our delectable Marketing Manager, Doreen?"

Babs coyly commented "I can't possibly say!" She had an uncanny way of confirming rumours without saying anything, strictly remaining loyal to her Mr Battle.

"That's un-discussable, Matthew." Daphne changed the tone of the conversation.

"Awww, come on, Daphy." Thomas tried.

"No, sorry. Particularly today – please, it's difficult. Say no more."

Daphne turned into the car park.

* * * * *

"Daphne, hi, it's Doreen. What's this meeting about?"

"Oh hi, Doreen, are you on your way?"

"Yes, but why haven't I got an agenda, and why the urgency? Is there a problem?"

Daphne was dreading this phone call. Doreen, after all, was more than a work colleague, but also a friend and they had, over the years, laughed over several gin and tonics about Doreen's exploits at her Sales Conferences – but this time she had gone too far.

"Oh, it's Dave's agenda. He will tell you when you get here."

"It sounds serious!"

"Drive carefully – see you soon."

* * * * *

"Morning, Dave. Daphne, what's up?" Dave and Daphne were sat together at one end of the Board table. Doreen's worst fears were about to be realised.

After talking to Daphne on the way in, Doreen had tried to work out what the issue could be. Doreen enjoyed the freedom of her external sales and marketing role and her 'full of life' character made the most of the conference facilities, overnight stays, the entertainment budget with suppliers and, of late, she had been spending a lot of time with the latest sales engineer recruit.

But all that's personal – it couldn't possibly be relevant, after all – sales are up, targets have been achieved and she had made a great presentation at the last Annual General Meeting.

"Have a seat, Doreen." Dave's tone was serious and Daphne wore a nervous smile.

"I'll come straight to the point. I've had a series of worrying reports about your behaviour."

"What? That's ridiculous!" Doreen began to feel sick. Nervous tension mounting, she just wanted to get out. "Who from? What about?"

"There are a number of issues – expenses and your behaviour at the York conference, and your relationship with Paul Pullyn, your recent addition to the Sales Team."

The conversation was difficult. Doreen defended herself strongly and managed to justify most of her expenses, but the real challenge was about to be addressed.

"Doreen, we know you are great fun and great to be with in a social crowd, but over the years, you have built up a reputation." Dave had spent all night rehearsing this interview, but suspected that he was just going to have to come out with it.

Daphne looked down, barely taking notes, and avoided eye contact with Doreen.

"Not all bad, Dave, you have to be outgoing and extrovert in this job!"

"Yes. However, your reputation of getting blind drunk and staying up with the boys till the early hours has had an impact on your credibility. You can't afford to be 'one of the boys' in your position."

Doreen turned pale, fearing the worst was yet to come. "And your relationship with Paul Pullyn?" Dave's mouth goes dry – he takes a gulp of his now cold coffee. "Is it true you knew him before he joined us?"

"Well, yes, sort of . . . ."

"OK, Doreen, I'll come straight to the point. It has come to my attention that you were having an affair with Paul before you recruited him. You are still having an affair. This came to my notice after one of our major customers phoned me last week after the York Conference, very concerned about your and Paul's behaviour. Sorry Doreen, but he saw you and Paul in a very compromising position on the snooker table, obviously drunk and . . . ."

Doreen broke down in tears.

* * * * *

The staff canteen bore little resemblance to the old, smoky, fatty-smelling, greasy spoon it used to be! Brightly coloured with new furnishings and a healthy eating menu with a sandwich bar. It not only gave good value for money, but was now running without subsidy.

"I love these cheese salad baps," Alison mumbled, barely holding on to the crumbs falling from her mouth.

"Give me a chip buttie any time!" Graham griped.

Alison and Graham had indeed buried the hatchet, not exactly in each other, but more drowned in pints of beer and cider one night. Since then, they had formed quite an alliance.

Alison enjoyed listening to the stories about the bad old days, and Graham, with an eye on semi-retirement was hoping to keep his hand in by delivering the occasional health and safety training session. He knew Alison could make this happen for him.

"So Graham, are you OK about how we progress with handling the warehouse shop issue?"

"As long as you have got the facts, then yes. I'll be there, but not representing him. I'll get another rep to do that."

At long last, for the first time that anyone can remember, the custom and practice of family and friends discounts on products sold at the shop was going to be confronted. It had never been a firm policy; it was always at the whim of whoever was serving.

It had only come to light through the increased scrutiny of accounts using the latest financial software. The obsessive Dick McKavit, the Finance Director, now insisted on regular, open and transparent reporting by all departments.

Graham was now well on board with the vision of the 'healing organisation'. To him, initially, it was all jargon and bullshit! Now, ever since he was given responsibility for reviewing Health and Safety as an improvement project working with a facilitator, his enjoyment and renewed enthusiasm for the business was tangible and visible for all who knew him previously as the grumpy, die-hard union official.

*　　*　　*　　*　　*

"A bit windy today, Ged – but good golf!"

"Yes, shame about the slow play." Ged takes another practice swing, waiting patiently.

"You're right, and it's time they were reported. They didn't even respond to my hint of letting us through at the last tee!" It didn't take much to wind Dave up on the golf course. Ged was a master at it, probably one of the reasons why he won most of the time.

"You can't report them Dave – it's the past Captain and guests."

"They did the same a few weeks ago, Ged. Everybody moans about them, but nobody ever seems to do anything about it!"

"Is it worth it Dave? Better to keep the peace."

"Bullshit Ged! I didn't get where I was today by keeping the peace!"

Indeed, it can be seen from our latest instalment that it takes courage and a will to follow through to confront difficult and sometimes undiscussable issues. It also takes wisdom to use your connections positively. In this chapter, we explore how we go beyond superficiality towards a long-lasting cure.

To do this, the 'shadowside' hidden or informal aspects of organisational life need to be identified and positively managed.

- Identify the shadows.
- Manage the shadows.

If you were to read this latest episode in Delectrex life in isolation, you might assume there were serious problems and that Delectix was showing the signs of a dysfunctional workplace. However, in the context of their programme of organisation development of healing, this is a healthy situation. Healthy because now there is courage and conviction to deal with long-standing, deep-seated issues that have become increasingly incongruous to the explicit 'healing' process that everyone is embarking upon.

The rumours, gossip, conversations between travel companions to and from work, the relationships, the social occasions, the talk and behaviours influenced by drink after conferences or training workshops are all natural parts of organisational life. Unfortunately, sometimes these get out of hand and need dealing with. The risk of not dealing with them leads to behaviours being tolerated and even seen as the 'norm'.

This can institutionalise sub-standard business or service practice. For example, turning a blind eye to selling company products with a large discount to friends and family can turn, over time, into custom and practice or unwritten policy.

It is even more difficult to challenge the behaviour of a senior manager, but essential to do so as this behaviour inadvertently gives the message that the behaviour is OK (in the case of Doreen, getting blind drunk at conferences).

It's not all negative, however. The relationship-building and catch-up created by work colleagues chatting on the journey to and from work or the honest heart-to-heart conversations over a social drink can resolve many issues and misunderstandings.

The nature of these events, because of their sensitivity and potential for causing problems, usually remains in the shadows – sometimes *so* hidden that they become undiscussable as it would be too painful and embarrassing to deal with the issue head on.

Any self-motivated healing process requires an honest look at oneself. To ask 'What's really going on?', 'What's stopping me reaching my full potential?', 'What am I blind to?' – and 'Can I face up to the truth?' These same questions are applicable to any organisation serious about developing a sustainable improvement culture (a healing organisation). World class organisations know themselves, inside and out – open and transparent practice, effective communication processes, no barriers due to hierarchy, profession or status and regular feedback from customers reduce the likelihood of blind spots and shadows becoming dysfunctional. It is also important to have effective audit and governance procedures and regular reviews of organisational values, asking the questions: 'Are we consistent with what we say we do and what we represent?' and 'Are we acting within an ethical code of practice?'

Identifying the shadows

To manage the shadowside of organisational life, first of all, you must recognise it. A good manager needs to understand how social and political life influences decision-making and resource allocation.

To illustrate examples of shadowside issues, I will use the categories usefully described by Gerard Egan in his book, *Working the Shadowside – A Guide to Positive Behind the Scenes Management.*[11] These are: organisational culture, personal styles, social systems, organisational politics and the hidden organisation.

Organisational culture

Culture simply means the 'way we do things around here'. Organisational culture is often visible and tangible in the way the people and working environment appears and feels. Here are three examples where the look and feel of a place give strong cultural indicators:

- Walking into Airflight Atlantic's head office, I was immediately confronted with a large moose head above the reception desk – celebrating their recent route to Vancouver. Walking around their offices, there was a buzz, an excitement, a casual and creative feel about the place.

- The Waste Water company depot was smart and clean, with health and safety notices everywhere. Their office was a little chaotic with piles of paper on desks and cardboard boxes with materials/brochures scattered about the floor.

- The management corridor of a large teaching hospital was long and dark. Every door was closed. Some had a sign which read 'Knock before Entering'.

---

[11] Egan, G., *Working the Shadowside – A Guide to Positive Behind the Scenes*, Management, Jossey Bass, 1994

There was a strong sense of hierarchy, i.e. the Chief Executive's office and Chairman's office was at the end. The only office door open was a secretary's at the beginning of the corridor – you got the distinct impression she was positioned to record the comings and goings.

You can see from the following three descriptions that some perceptions of culture can be easily made:

Airflight Atlantic: surprising, informal, creative.

Waste Water: efficient at operational level, chaotic at management level.

Teaching Hospital: hierarchical, imposing, closed.

How would you describe *your* company culture?

The culture becomes relevant and critical for those wishing to become a 'healing organisation'. The values, beliefs and norms will drive the culture. You need to ask yourself whether the current values, beliefs and norms are consistent with the vision you describe for the future success of your company, department or team.

My job in the large teaching hospital was 'Director of Organisational Development'. The reason I was hired was to help lead and shape culture change. I decided that one way to make my mark was to be different, so one day, instead of wearing the usual dark suit, which was the norm in the 'top corridor' as it was called, I chose to wear slacks, no tie and a blazer. One morning, walking down the corridor with no windows, I came face to face with the newly appointed Chairman, who happened to be the retired Chairman of a major clothing retail company. He stopped, looked me up and down and said 'Dressing down today are you, Mr Wash?' then he walked away shaking his head. What did I do?

The following day, I arrived at work in the customary uniform – dark suit. I decided this culture will not change by confronting it. I was going to have to work with it from the inside.

---

46. Talk to the 'shadows'. Be clear about the culture you want and what is acceptable and what's not acceptable.

The right background, social class, qualifications, or even the way you dress, can influence the way you are treated – depending on how congruent you are with the culture.

For example, the nursing profession in the UK has become increasingly academically oriented. The former 'Enrolled Nurse' qualification has become unacceptable and only 'Registration' is seen as the real qualification – moreover, a *degree*-based nursing qualification is needed if chances of promotion are going to be realistic. As a nurse tutor, if you didn't have a degree, you are second class. To what extent does professional arrogance and snobbery get in the way of judging people for what they can actually do?

In today's working climate, where diversity is encouraged, one must ask, to what extent does prejudice interfere with our communication, decision-making, career development and team ethos. Without asking this question, prejudice can begin to be institutionalised – ceasing to be recognised or acknowledged as a problem from within. It becomes the norm. Large institutions are particularly at risk (e.g. Health Service, Military, Police, etc.).

While running a team-building event for a high security psychiatric hospital, I was helping them review some of their work practices. They were describing what could only be described as 'a punishment' regime for certain difficult patients.

I showed my surprise and asked, 'Are you sure that's right? It seems a little inhumane?' They then described a whole range of practices that had been going on for years and years, and when asked 'Would you be happy to know your mother or father, or some other member of your family, was being treated this way?', they quickly realised with the confirming input of someone who had recently joined the team that they had institutionalised sub-standard practice. Over the years, it had become the norm, part of the culture. The newest member of the team was too keen to make an impression and too frightened to speak out. It took an external facilitator to get them to take an honest look in the mirror.

So many cases of prolonged malpractice have resulted in often quite tragic cases of abuse. In some cases it can result in the tragic loss of life. The Piper Alpha Oil Rig disaster in 1988, where 167 men died, was partly due to fear culture and adversarial relationships developed between managers and the unions, resulting in a reluctance to report faulty readings when shifts were changing. The consequences were horrendous.

The culture of winning and securing multi-million dollar contracts and the lack of management courage to confront this was partly the reason why seven astronauts died in the Challenger explosion in 1986. The now infamous 'O' ring default was deemed to be a risk worth taking given the financial consequence of delaying the whole programme.

More recently, and closer to home, the custom and practice of taking children's organs for research after they died was no more evident than in Alder Hey Children's Hospital pathology department. Although this was the case highlighted and publicised, it was in fact custom and practice to a certain extent in many hospitals.

How do these things happen? Shadows become darker, issues become sensitive, individuals build walls, and before long it becomes too difficult to confront and it's easier to keep the peace or pretend it is not happening.

A common defence is to deny responsibility – 'it's not my job', 'it's not my department' or 'I am not senior enough to challenge it'.

For organisations to heal, everyone needs to care about what ever goes on in the organisation, to the extent that if something is wrong, they 'speak out'.

Some questions to help you explore your own culture are:

- What are the dominant values that drive your organisation?
- What standards are actually really acceptable?
- What background or social class will get more positive social attention?
- What standard of appearance is preferred?
- What prejudices influence the way we work together?
- What are the major discrepancies between what the organisation espouses (said policy) and actually does (done policy)?
- How do we make the current culture work for us?
- What is our desired culture?

Personal styles

In every organisation I have worked in, there have always been characters that are 'larger than life'. They add colour, intrigue and challenge. Managing 'characters' is difficult, partly because they are often good at what they do, despite the impact they may have on people around them, and partly because they are often liked, sociable or maintain an 'ego' so big it would take real courage to confront.

In our fictional company, Doreen's behaviour was never confronted – partly because she was good at her job and really fun to be with. However, being the life and soul of the party can be a disguise as I found to my cost when working for a community hospital in Scotland. One of the facilitators happened to be a comedian. He was the joker of the pack. Every opportunity he got to add humour, he would, and he was popular, sociable and easy to be with. During his training, he gave no indication that in effect he was very sceptical about the value of what we were doing, and behind our backs he was 'bad-mouthing' the whole process. This 'act' or 'disguise' was costing the organisation – wasting time in training,

189

reducing motivation and commitment of others while working on projects. It wasn't until, during a facilitator meeting, someone challenged him on his attitude, that it became clear what lay behind the 'humour'. It concluded in an honest discussion about his reservation and confidence. He stopped 'bad-mouthing'.

Somehow, people start to believe that they have a right to misbehave or demand attention, that they have priority, or are a law unto themselves – often as a result of a strong sense of belief that they are good at what they do. Their egos tell them the organisation is lucky to have them, and therefore they deserve preferential treatment.

---

47. Have the courage to challenge long-standing, dysfunctional and previously undiscussable issues.

Characters I have worked with include a world famous surgeon who believed nurses and managers were the servants of doctors, a car-dealer principal who kept a machine gun mounted on his desk in case he had someone in front of him giving him 'bullshit', a manager who managed his team through a drugged and drunken haze, a marketing manager who continually sent abusive messages around the company about his chief executive, an engineering manager who continually fell asleep at almost every meeting, a nursing manager who used to moonlight as a pole-dancer, a finance manager who ran two other companies at the same time, using the accounts to evade tax, a genius senior planning manager who was a bully and 'bad-mouthed' anything that wasn't his idea, and many more.

These individuals got away with their behaviour for years. It's important to harness the energy and enthusiasm of 'characters' in a positive way. Being clear about what is acceptable and what is not acceptable is only fair to the individual and the organisation.

We could probably eliminate the cost of employee theft, but it is difficult to eliminate the cost of arrogance or incompetence of some key players.

What style of leadership dominates your organisation? What are the positive and negative aspects of this? Are you handling your characters positively?

---

48. Harness the enthusiasm of your characters and key players; manage them positively.

Social systems

A healthy healing culture is one where many social needs are met at work. Knowing each other as people with hobbies and interests outside of work, family and social events are important. Social cohesion between people enhances morale and team work. However, when these social systems become exclusive and hidden, potential shadows can create resentment, jealousy, suspicion and conflict.

Here are some social systems at work where members are part of the 'in-crowd' and, potentially, able to influence decisions and relationships at work.

- The lunch time 'three card brag' card school (nurses only)
- The Mah-jong club (Chinese members only)
- The snooker club (no managers allowed)
- The golf tournament (engineers only)
- The pub after work for a drink (Operational Directors' favoured few)
- The breakfast club (clique of managers before work starts – table reserved)
- The bridge club (Chief Executive, Finance Director, Estate Director and Wife)
- Buscom (key managers travelling together to and from work on the same bus)

In the above list, I was only ever a member of one group (the 'three card brag' card school). I was invited to two others but declined (the pub after work and the engineers golf tournament).

The others, I was told, were the places where real decisions were made.

> **49. Encourage the inclusive social activities. Be wise to the exclusive cliques and clubs.**

The positive aspect of engendering a social, friendly environment at work relates to team-building and motivation. The negative aspect, if left to develop for its own sake, is that it can distract from work (talking about family, home, weekend/holiday exploits, chat rooms, online, emailing social chat while supposedly at work) – but worse, the group/team can become so inward-looking that they become isolated and start thinking they are better than others, blaming other teams or departments for failures and before long, a 'them and us' climate or tribal warfare between departments becomes part of the culture.

The wise manager will know of the social groups, will balance socialising at work appropriately and provide inclusive social opportunities to be together.

Who are the in-groups, out-groups, cliques, tribes and warring factors?

Where, outside of meetings/work time, does real influence and decision-making occur?

Organisational politics

Politics in this context relates to the use and abuse of power. Who do you think holds the power? Well, you would be right in thinking that formal power is clearly in the hands of the executive team and the Board; however, informal power can be held by anyone in a position of influence.

In my naivety and enthusiasm, I decided to purchase some notebooks from a local stationer as the type I wanted was not available on the hospital stationery list. Several weeks later, I was confronted by the irate Chief Executive's secretary. 'How dare you purchase stationery without me knowing – all purchases on this corridor must come through me!'

I did not handle this exchange well – it took months, plus a box of chocolates and a bunch of flowers for her to start seeing me as an ally, rather than an enemy. To my cost, she was the gate-keeper to the boss so my papers for him to comment on were delayed; it was very difficult to get an appointment, and sometimes my messages or requests were mysteriously forgotten.

Lesson? Never upset the Chief Executive's secretary/PA – potentially, one of the most powerful individuals in the organisation. Invariably, they know everything that's going on and can pick their moment to apply their influence.

Professional power can be used as a case for resisting change or demanding resource. Pilots and Hospital Consultants are two formidable forces. They can easily hold an organisation to ransom based on their professional power.

These dynamics remain in the shadows because the nature of informal power is covert. Used as and when necessary. Other examples include the Finance Director who makes his 'art' so mysterious that no-one really knows what money is available, the Health and Safety manager who supports and quotes legal detail every time his favourite team want to bid for more resource, the solicitor who happens to be a friend of the Chancellor (getting preferred cases), the HR director who knows one or two 'dark secrets' and uses them to extract favours.

Again, use and abuse of power is a natural part of organisational life. Using this power in the context of positive leadership and influence is the aim, but be wary of the abuse of power and ask why it is necessary to use. What's wrong with the formal channels of influencing and decision-making? Power, abuse and calling in favours are sometimes encouraged by over-bureaucratic and outdated policies and systems.

Who holds the power in your organisation? How is this used to protect or build empires? How can you harness individuals or professional power positively?

> **50. Manage all stakeholders wisely, use the power of positive politics and influence to gain commitment and support for your vision. Understand the objectives of key stakeholders and how they relate to your own.**

Hidden organisation

Some people just have the knack of getting their own way, or is it about having the wherewithall to manipulate policy and systems to your own advantage? More than likely, it's to do with having friends and contacts in positions of influence, who can speed requests, decisions or approvals through – bypassing the usual formal channels. This happens all the time, from parliamentary questions to getting personal expenses approved quicker than usual. 'Making that call', 'you scratch my back, I'll scratch yours' and 'let's look after our own' are all phrases used to justify bypassing formal procedure to get the result you want. How is it that new people arrive when there is supposed to be a recruitment freeze, how come only a few company car renewals were approved, why did it take me three months to get a new laptop and you got one the day after you requested it? You will find the answer to these questions lie in 'it's not what you know, but who you know that has clout around here'. These issues can become dysfunctional shadows if they engender resentment and accusation of inequality and mistrust. The credibility of formal power and policy could be threatened. It is important therefore to ask if the formal systems are efficient, fair and transparent. Also, it's good to have some open flexibility for special cases or urgent demands.

A project I was involved in with a large telecommunications company created a major shift in the way telecom engineers worked.

Each morning, telecom engineers used to pick up their order for installations and repairs to residential homes. They placed each 'pick' of order in their van and arrived at the address to install or repair, but alas – more often than not – it was the wrong set of equipment or something was missing. Over the years, the engineers, not wanting to disappoint the customer or waste time going back and forth to the stores, began to accumulate their own 'spares'. After a while, each engineers' van had a rich collection of spares and each corner of every telecom yard had a cupboard of further stores (just in case).

All this developed because of the lack of confidence the engineers had in the central store systems. On the surface, no harm was being done and the customers remained satisfied. However, much of the accumulated stock was not only out of date, but was increasingly being used in a thriving engineers' private business of putting extra phones and sockets in for 'cash in hand'. This, of course, was costing the company millions. The analysis related to this project resulted in a powerful business case for a complete revamp of the central store systems.

This syndrome of holding surplus stock because of low confidence in requesting renewals to be delivered on time and being available when you want them is not unusual.

How many offices have their own secret and surplus supply of stationery? How many departments in hospitals lock up their own wheelchairs and other aids to ensure no-one else uses them?

All these methods are covert, hidden to the untrained eye and can be very costly to the organisation.

How many budget holders do their best to spend up before the year end, fearful of their annual case for an increased budget being weakened. I remember when I was a Charge Nurse in a large psychiatric hospital, the unit manager came round to ask for requests for new furniture. I said we didn't need any. He disagreed and proceeded to use the flimsiest excuses to replace perfectly good tables and chairs. If he didn't, he could be accused of having asked for too much budget in the first place, so next time round his budget would be cut. I believe this departmentalised budget protection still goes on today – a symptom of not buying into the bigger picture. They want to be stone cutters with ample supply of stones, rather than Cathedral Builders.

The trust and confidence in sharing and managing resources collectively often is not there, especially in large companies and service institutions.

How are systems and procedures bypassed to get things done in your organisation?

Managing the shadows

Many organisations attempt to implement programmes of change. Unfortunately, they become short-lived initiatives and fall well short of achieving 'healing organisation' status. There are many reasons for this, but the most common and substantial is the inability to deal with the embedded dysfunctional attitudes and behaviours that are often reinforced in the shadows, or undiscussable.

The odds are stacked against any organisation wanting to embark upon culture change as the human tendency to resist and defend their position is a natural one. The following is taken from *54 Approaches to Managing Change at Work*, pages 14-15.

Inner (statements about self)

- Lack of confidence.
- Perception of poor self-ability, lack of or inappropriate skill.
- Fear of the unknown.
- Familiarity and comfort in old ways of working.
- Security of past and present.
- Tiredness, stress, or other physical reasons for not changing.
- I like myself as I am.
- No need to change.
- If I change, what happens to the relationships I have?
- I'm too old for this game.
- I need more experience before the next step.
- I need to finish what I am doing first and learn from it before I try anything new.
- It's all too risky; I might fail or be rejected.
- I'm not senior enough to challenge the powers that be.

Outer (statements about others, or reasons given for not changing)

- This company is proud of its tradition and has built its reputation on solid and sound virtues.
- We need to be convinced of the operational value before risking new development.
- We have no confidence in the proposed changes or in its top-down imposition, and we are not involved, so we will continue to do our own thing.
- It costs too much money.
- Our priorities at the moment are productivity, shareholder satisfaction, and meeting deadlines, so don't talk about change now.
- The boss won't wear it.
- It may have worked there, but we are different.
- It's all been tried before.
- Interesting proposal – let me have more details before I decide whether to have a steering committee on this or not.
- Sorry, no resources.
- This is not your concern.
- I don't trust you.
- Do you realise the legal implications and complexities of this?
- At another time, this proposal would be very appropriate.

These resistances are often disguised in what can be referred to as 'defensive routines'. In his book, *Overcoming Organizational Defences*, C. Argyris offered the following definition of defensive routines:

"Defensive routines are probably the most important cause of failure in the implementation of sound strategy, regardless of the approach used. Defensive routines are actions that are designed to reduce the individual's or the organisation's pain, and when used effectively, they prevent correcting the causes of pain. Defensive routines reduce pain and simultaneously inhibit learning."[12]

> ### 51. Check that all policies, systems and procedures are serving the business, ensure bypassing is not the norm.

Some examples of these are:

Projection

- Inability to recognise own part or role in the creation of unproductive situations – blaming others or the systems.
- Expressing negative thoughts and feelings to someone or something other than the cause of those thoughts and feelings – for example:

"The Director has given me a bad time, so don't think you're going to get off lightly."

Reverting back to type

- Reverting back to well and tried behaviour that had payoffs in the past – especially in difficult, confusing and new situations – for example:

A Manager tries facilitating, frustration builds and he concludes with directing and deciding without consideration of the group's discussions.

Rationalisation

- Finding good reasons for present behaviour, decisions – for example:

  – *Useful for the meeting to go overtime as it was a difficult topic and uncovered some important issues*

---

[12] Argyris, C., *Overcoming Organizational Defences*, Prentice Hall, 1990

- *if I had achieved all of my objectives this year, next year would have been even more difficult, so I'm pleased with my performance so far*
- *if I had got that promotion, it would have probably created more difficulties than I would want to handle anyway*

Compensation

- What I lack in people management, I more than make up for in my knowledge and expertise in finance.

Denial

- This job is 'too much' probably because I'm not feeling very well, therefore 'off sick'.
- Memory lapse for difficult or anxious situations.

The consequence of not managing the shadowside issues is likely to be 'status quo'. See Figure 16.

Shadows are a reality of organisational life and, ideally, they should serve the business. The leadership agenda in promoting 'healing' at every level needs to be one of positive politics and efficient, open management practice.

The key areas to enable positive politics and effective shadowside management are:

- Effective problem-solving and project management
- Management by fact
- Double loop learning
- Challenging skills
- Stakeholder analysis

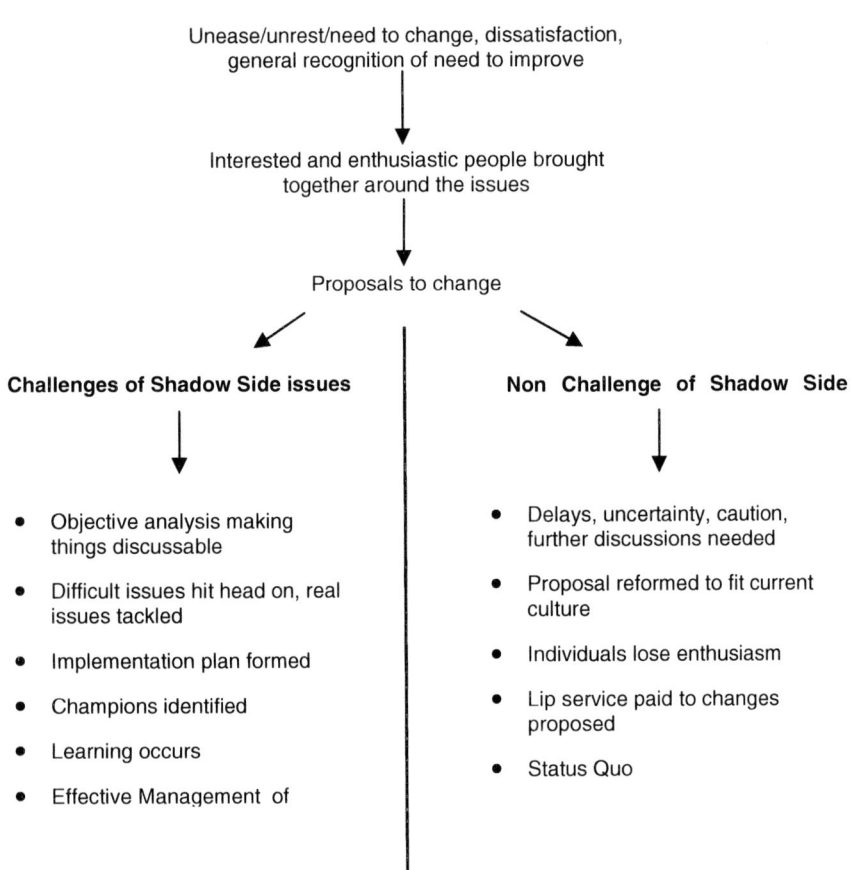

Figure 16. Why manage the shadowside?

Effective problem-solving

Chapter 2 describes a process of empowerment. This process, when applied to problem-solving and project management, encourages the root cause of problems and barriers to be identified and harnesses team strength to challenge resistance and defensive routines.

For each step in the process, a 'shadowside' challenge may be needed to ensure the right issues are being addressed.

Step 1	What's going on?	Don't accept hear-say – get hard facts and the data from a wide variety of sources.
Step 2	What's really going on?	Challenge the data, go deeper. Ask why and ask what's missing?
Step 3	Identify key issues	Chose the issue that, when addressed, is going to make the biggest difference, no matter how tough it may be.
Step 4	Create a vision	Be positive, believe in yourself and your organisation. Don't accept 'yes, but . . . .' – challenge negativity.
Step 5	Set goals	Make sure they are SMARTER and outcome focused. If actions are proposed – ask what are they trying to achieve to get more outcome focused?
Step 6	Test commitment	Challenge the heart as well as the mind. How motivated are people in following this through?
Step 7	Brainstorm actions	Don't accept a shortlist – go for a long list. Give people freedom and permission to be creative and wild with their ideas.
Step 8	Shortlist best actions	Focus down on the actions that will be immediate and have a positive effect.
Step 9	Plan	Gain commitment for action. This usually means behaviour and time commitment diarised.

Each step, as described, contains a challenge. This challenge will, if presented in the context of making explicit organisation values, will begin to address what may be intractable, deep seated organisational problems.

Management by fact

In the absence of information or facts, we are left to assume. Management by guessing or inferring what's going on is commonplace. Rumours, gossip and the grapevine feed this tendency and the thrill of exploring possibilities will never lose its' attraction.

This can become dysfunctional, especially when the level of assumption is far removed from fact, but still used to influence decisions and relationships. Chris Argyris describes this process by illustrating the 'ladder of inference':

Level 1	Observable facts.	'John has drunk 4 glasses of water this morning.'
Level 2	Generally understood meaning.	'John must be thirsty.'
Level 3	Meanings imposed by us.	'He's probably got a hangover!'
Level 4	Theories we use to create the measuring or justify on level 3.	'I wonder if he has a drink problem?'

The above example can, and often does, develop a further two levels. Level 5 being 'He has a drink problem because he is stressed' and Level 6 becomes 'I suspect this is a bad organisation to work for'.

Another example:

Level 1	Chief Executive declares a recruitment freeze.
Level 2	Things are tough, finances tight.
Level 3	We are at serious risk as a business.
Level 4	Redundancies are next (the rumours start flying!)

We can see from the above example that if a recruitment freeze is announced without adequate explanation, then escalation to Level 4 can quickly feed the defensive responses of staff union representatives, and before long, meetings in the shadows begin to plan industrial action.

However, it could surely be explained that temporary recruitment freezes are not uncommon when taking stock in an uncertain economical situation.

So, ask the questions; what's really going on, what are the facts, let's hear them first hand, what can we see, what's the data, what is the tangible information we have? By minimising assumption (which can make as **ASS** of **U** and **ME**) there is more chance of lightening the shadows.

> **52. Manage by fact, challenge assumptions, share knowledge to become the 'intelligent' organisation.**

More on the 'Ladder of Inference' can be read in *54 Tools and Techniques for Business Excellence,* Technique N° 4, page 26.

Double loop learning

Single loop learning refers to the process when we make an adjustment or change as a consequence of feedback. Double loop learning goes a little deeper in asking the questions:

- What chain of events led up to us making the mistake in the first place?
- What values and assumptions contributed to the cause?
- What can we learn about preventing this in the future?
- How do we reduce our vulnerability?

These types of searching questions are likely to uncover root causes, which can be hidden deep in the shadows. Better to ask them as part of an established review process in-house than to be on the receiving end of an external investigation.

Argyris and Schone, (1978) describe this in the context of Organisational Learning. The process is illustrated in Figure 17.

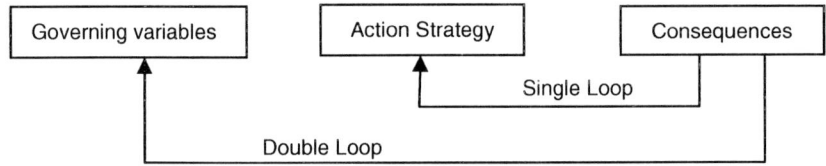

Figure 17. Double loop learning

Argyris and Schone's proposition is that single loop learning may correct and improve the presenting situation, but unless the searching questions relating to contributing factors or governing variables are asked, then the chances of reoccurrence of the problem is high. By reviewing the governing variables, challenges to the current values, norms, systems and processes can happen.

This is important in any review and helps minimise the 'blame culture' as it highlights the fact that no-one acts in isolation, and invariably, there is a contributory chain of events leading up to the incident. These chains of events need to be brought out of the shadows if long-lasting healing is to be achieved.

The skills for challenging

Challenging another person is powerful medicine. Necessary if discrepant or dysfunctional behaviour is to be highlighted and stopped. However, there are two significant reasons why 'challenging skills' are not typically a strong competency in management:

- Reluctance to challenge others.
- Perception as confrontation rather than a positive opportunity to learn.

Finding out what's really going on, often in the darkest corners of organisational life, requires strong challenging skills. However, because this is such a 'strong medicine', these skills need to be skilfully conveyed on a basis of trust, rapport and understanding. One must first earn the right to challenge by demonstrating empathy.

> **53. Learn from mistakes; challenge the chain of events causing incidents and transform weaknesses to strengths.**

If you are reluctant, hesitant or shy away from engaging in difficult, challenging conversation, where you may have to give 'bad news', then ask yourself the following:

Are any of these expressions relevant to your experience or what you think/fear or believe?

- 'The bearer of bad news.' (May get shot).
- 'Fear of hurting someone's feelings or creating some form of emotional damage.'
- 'Uncovering an area that would be too difficult to handle.'
- 'Reluctance to get close to someone.'
- 'Fear of rejection.'
- 'Wanting to be liked.'
- 'Being rejected or hurt in the past yourself and therefore not wanting to repeat the experience for someone else.'
- 'Can't afford the emotional investment – just too difficult – easier to avoid or ignore.'
- 'Fear of reprisal.'
- 'Fear of breaking friendship or trust.'

The above may give you clues for your own development. Some guidance as to how to challenge effectively is captured in the following hints and tips:

- Helping individuals recognise what they can and can't influence – encourage their ownership when they tell their story.
- Be a mirror to reflect back the discrepancy between what someone says and does.
- Listen to the full story and summarise back helping the individual to pick out themes or links.
- Be prepared to discuss potential barriers between you (immediacy), and talk through 'baggage' (things in the past that have caused problems).
- Listen between the lines, observe non-verbal communication, and play your hunch (tentatively) that maybe there is something not said – or something else going on.
- You may need to give some factual information to help someone see things from a different perspective.

More detail about challenging skills can be found in *54 Tools and Techniques for Business Excellence*.

Stakeholder analysis

There are many people right now who have a vested interest in what you are doing. Some are more important than others, either because of their potential influence on what you do, or you value their feedback.

When things don't go to plan, or there is a setback in gaining someone's approval, or you get surprised by objections – it's time to see what dynamics, relationships and agendas were dancing in the shadows. It is better to join in and dance in these shadows to find out what is going on, before you present a proposal for change or implement a new system, etc.

Stakeholder analysis is a technique that helps bring this complex web of inter-related influences alive. Refer to *54 Tools and Techniques for Business Excellence,* Technique N° 6, page 32.

By mapping these connections out and judging how each individual or group relates to what you are trying to achieve, you begin to get an indication of who you should influence first and how. Use positive politics in persuading a foe to become an ally. The following list of stakeholder categories is useful when deciding how people relate to what you are trying to achieve.

Partners	Joint responsibility.
Allies	Trust and respect.
Fellow travellers	Similar agenda, can learn from.
Fence sitters	Don't know which way to go.
Loose cannons	Unpredictable and dangerous.
Opponents	Disagree with agenda.
Adversaries	Disagree with you.
Bedfellows	Support agenda; maybe you.
The voiceless	Will be affected; passive resistance if not involved.
Victims	Have already been hurt.
Missionaries	Enthusiastic for any change.
Early adopters	Willing to test out ideas.

Another useful framework is to identify the extent to which they have power and interest. See Figure 18.

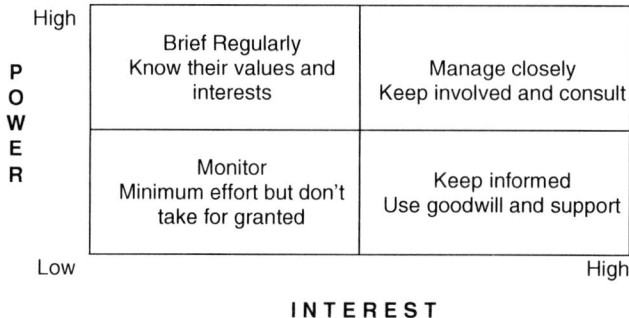

Figure 18. Stakeholder commitment

Managing stakeholders is essential if you are to bring multiple, potentially conflicting, agendas out into the open. You can't 'heal' on your own. You need an army of supportive, interested and influential people at every level in the organisation.

It is time to bring the corridor, bus and toilet conversations out into the open. Better to deal with difficult issues as they arise, before they go into the shadows, or worse still – become undiscussable.

Finally

The focus of this 'healing' journey has been about how to harness the potential of everyone in the organisation to create sustainable excellence within a healthy working environment.

Leaders today have a responsibility to see the bigger picture. Not only should they respect the fact that each staff member has a life outside the workplace; they should also recognise that the life outside is also a leadership concern.

Today's global market and economy challenges today's leaders' scope of responsibility. Any organisation at any time can be under threat from disease, virus and sabotage – e.g. pandemics, fuel and energy prices, over-lending, bad debt, war, terrorism, customer loss of confidence.

The healthier the organisation, the greater the chance to sustain excellence through adversity. Global responsible leadership will require a sharing of best practice, agreement of ethics and standards as to how, by working together, the healing process can go beyond traditional company boundaries.

For too long, organisations have worked in isolation, over-concerned with attacking the competition and protecting itself.

The global challenge is one that opens the possibility of organisations contributing to a global healing process. A process where investment in third-world economies is not seen as charity, but one where the resources given are directed in such a way that creates sustainability within the context of cultural need and independence.

The principles and processes of the 'healing organisation' can be applied to any community that has a desire to change. It will require leadership, facilitation, focus, training, care and wise and sensitive work in the shadows.

The principles remain the same whether it is a manufacturing business, a hospital, a school or a community project: create the environment where individuals feel free to contribute to a worthwhile goal.

Recognise their strengths, value their contribution, respect differences in an air of creativity, fun and productivity.

One of my strongest desires and hopes for this world is that somehow the politics of self-interest are transformed into the politics of global healing.

> **54. See the bigger picture, go beyond organisation boundaries, contribute to community and global healing.**

About the Author

I have been in the business of helping individuals and organisations realise their full potential for over 20 years.

My early career as a psychiatric nurse gave me great fascination and insight into the extremes of human behaviour. I progressed my career to teaching psychiatry, psychology and counselling within the UK Health Service. During this period, I also qualified as a psychotherapist, and co-authored a best-selling text book, *Psychiatric Nursing Skills – A client centred approach*, first published by Chapman Hall in 1986 (second edition published in 2000 by Nelson Thornes).

I became restless within my teaching position and began questioning whether my skills and experience could be applied elsewhere, as at the time, in the early 80s – the Health Service seemed to be a gigantic and less than dynamic monolith, and I was ready to spread my wings.

I wrote a paper with the proposition that senior executives in large organisations were probably deluded at best, and at worst, psychotic – given that very few could possibly understand the impact they had on others. This paper gave me several interviews, one of which led to a job offer which transformed my working and personal life. I became a member of the internal consulting team in British Telecom.

Here I learnt my business acumen, dovetailing my caring, teaching and counselling skills to an organisation agenda desperate for change. During this period, I also completed my Masters Degree in Business and Economics, researching the effectiveness of leadership behaviour in service industry.

After 5 years on a very steep learning curve, it became apparent that I was best suited as a free agent – I left and set up my own business in 1989.

Apart from 2 years employed as an Organisation Development Director for a large teaching hospital, my work has primarily been consulting to organisations whose quest included how to recover from crisis, how to build a team, how to transform an organisation and how to change a culture from one that is holding back performance to one that becomes a self sustainable healing culture, working toward world class standards.

I have had the privilege of working with many great organisations and enjoyed the freedom and vulnerability of the travelling consultant. I can't envisage a time when I will tire from working with those people who have a thirst and passion to change, learn, improve and realise their ambition for a better way of working and a healthier, balanced lifestyle, for themselves and the community they serve.

Other Publications by Michael Wash

54 Approaches to Managing Change at Work (2nd ed)
Published 2009 by Management Books 2000

Have you ever wondered why it is so hard to get people to buy in to what seems to be a sensible, or even brilliant, new idea or way of doing things?

Have you ever felt a little uneasy or unsettled when asked to do something new or change something you have been doing for years?

Have you ever wondered why people react in many sometimes strange, and obstructive, ways to events at work – that should be seen as work?

Have you ever had self doubt about presenting something that maybe new or challenging to your audience?

In this book, I have tried to illustrate the varied approaches (sometime not effective) that people adopt to get others to do things they may initially resist. These approaches also challenge the reader to look at themselves and their own willingness to be open to change.

The situations cover many work-related (some would say life-related) incidents, such as redundancy, stress, imposed new systems, change of job, bullying, promotion and many more.

In addition to these are exercises to give you feedback on your effectiveness in managing your personal development, time management, meeting effectiveness and how you work as a team. A questionnaire on leadership will help you gain insight into your own style of influencing others.

Every manager and supervisor should read this book and if your organisation has courage, and wants to create a healthy, thriving work environment, then pass the book on to your staff and ask them to choose an approach which they would like to discuss!!

Good luck in dismantling your brickwalls!

54 Tools and Techniques for Business Excellence
Published 2007 by Management Books 2000

This book will be of great value to anyone interested in improving their personal, team or organisational business performance. It is simple and practical to use, with handy hints and tips for success. It includes thought-provoking exercises and questions to use with your colleagues. The tools and techniques in this book have been tried and tested in some of the world's best companies. From the simplest 'generation of ideas' to the 'transformation of organisational culture', these tools and techniques are the essential basics – the 'must do' and the 'must know' of management and business excellence.

"The book is full of simple, useful and practical examples for change practitioners of any background. It is based on real life examples of problems and deals with human and emotional intelligence issues as well as the system and process matters. Junior and middle managers, together with anyone embarking on a process of change, will benefit from this book."
Tony Bell OBE, Chief Executive Officer, Royal Liverpool Children's Hospital

"I like the simplicity and presentation of the material. Mike has managed to provide a succinct summary of each technique that is instantly usable to a 'newcomer' or that rekindles the memory spark for experienced practitioners."
Malcolm Hurrell, Vice President, Human Resources, AstraZeneca

"Mike's exceptional interpersonal effectiveness and skills in change management are made accessible to busy executives in this very practical guide – an ideal resource for the challenges of getting strategy into action."
Graham Barkus, Manager Learning and Development Group and Head of Training and Development, Cathay Pacific Airways

Also Available: **54 Simple Truths with Brutal Advice – How to face the challenges of life** (via www.54simpletruths-with-brutaladvice.com)